MW01285314

64 GAME-DAY RECIPES
INSPIRED BY EVERY
PRO FOOTBALL TEAM

TIM LOPEZ

EPIC INK

© 2025 by Quarto Publishing Group USA Inc.

First published in 2025 by Epic Ink, an imprint of The Quarto Group,
142 West 36th Street, 4th Floor, New York, NY 10018, USA
(212) 779-4972 www.Quarto.com

All rights reserved. No part of this book may be reproduced in any form without written
permission of the copyright owners. All images included in this book are original
works created by the artist credited on the copyright page, not generated by artificial
intelligence, and have been reproduced with the knowledge and prior consent of the
artist. The producer, publisher, and printer accept no responsibility for any infringement
of copyright or otherwise arising from the contents of this publication. Every effort has
been made to ensure that credits accurately comply with the information supplied. We
apologize for any inaccuracies that may have occurred and will address inaccurate
or missing information in a subsequent reprinting of the book.

Epic Ink titles are also available at discount for retail, wholesale, promotional,
and bulk purchase. For details, contact the Special Sales Manager by email at
specialsales@quarto.com or by mail at The Quarto Group, Attn: Special Sales Manager,
100 Cummings Center Suite 265D, Beverly, MA 01915 USA.

10 9 8 7 6 5 4 3 2 1

ISBN: 978-0-7603-9703-9

Digital edition published in 2025
eISBN: 978-0-7603-9704-6

Library of Congress Control Number: 2025936536

Group Publisher: Rage Kindelsperger
Editorial Director: Erin Canning
Creative Director: Laura Drew
Photo Art Director: Marisa Kwek
Managing Editor: Cara Donaldson
Editor: Katie McGuire
Text: Tim Lopez
Cover and Interior Design: Casey Schuurman
Food Photography: Elysa Weitala
Food Styling: Victoria Woollard
Food Stylist Assistants: Allee Cakmis & Penny Eng
Props: Alessandra Mortola & Elysa Weitala
Food Photo, Page 97: Shutterstock
Food Photo, Page 141: Cathy Scola/Getty Images

Printed in China

This publication has not been prepared, approved, or licensed by the author, producer,
or owner of any motion picture, television program, book, game, blog, or other work
referred to herein. This is not an official or licensed publication. We recognize further
that some words, models' names, and designations mentioned herein are the property of
the trademark holder. We use them for identification purposes only. Resources for Team
Tidbits available upon request.

This book is dedicated to all NFL fans. They understand that every stadium has a story and every city has its own unique flavor. It is these diverse flavors that make each city a champion in its own right. May these recipes bring that spirit into your kitchen.

CONTENTS ★

AFC

NFC

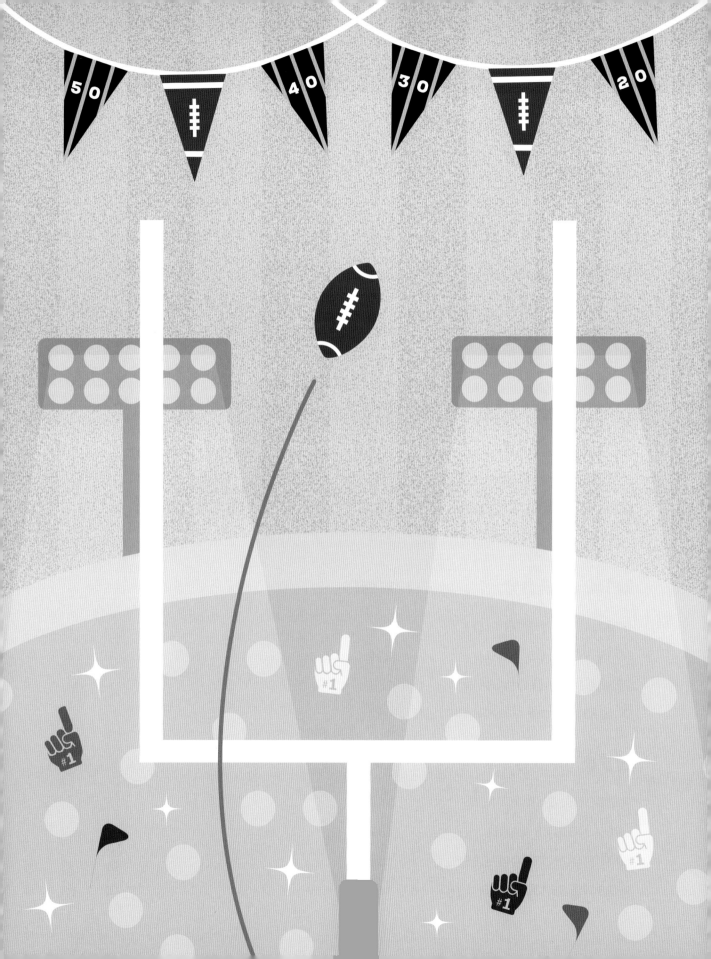

INTRODUCTION

Football is more than just a game—it's a cultural phenomenon that unites cities, sparks fierce rivalries, and brings communities together every Sunday. Just as each team has its own history, traditions, and loyal fan base, every region of the country has a distinct food culture that reflects its people, geography, and heritage. From the smoky barbecue pits of Kansas City to the seafood shacks of New England, the food that fuels football fans is as diverse and passionate as the sport itself.

This cookbook is a tribute to that culinary spirit. The recipes within have been painstakingly gathered from local markets, family kitchens, and beloved hometown eateries, ensuring that each dish represents the authentic flavors of the NFL's thirty-two teams. Whether it's the hearty, nostalgic comfort food of the North, the bold, spice-laden dishes of the South, the fresh, innovative flavors of the West, or the iconic classics of the East, every meal tells a story about the people who cheer from the stands, tailgate in the parking lots, and break bread together watching at home.

By truly exploring the food culture of football, you gain a deeper understanding of the passion that fuels fans across the country. These dishes aren't just meals—they're traditions, shared experiences, and expressions of regional pride. With an appetizer and entrée dedicated to each team, this cookbook offers a flavorful journey through the cities and states that make up the NFL. Whether you're cooking up a feast for game day or simply looking to experience the regional tastes of your game-day rival, each recipe brings you closer to the appetites and enthusiasm of football fans nationwide.

So, fire up your grills and ovens, set the table, and get ready to experience the flavors of football. No matter which team you root for, one thing is certain—you are going to eat well!

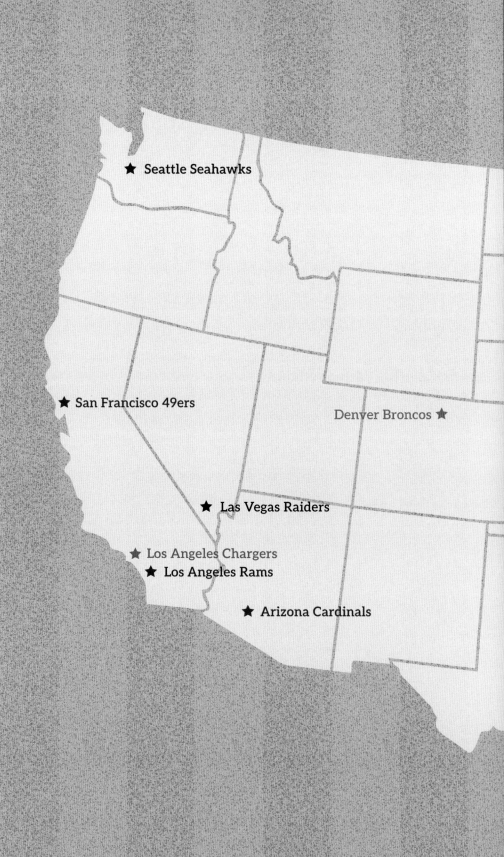

Seattle Seahawks ★

★ San Francisco 49ers

Denver Broncos ★

★ Las Vegas Raiders

★ Los Angeles Chargers
★ Los Angeles Rams

★ Arizona Cardinals

★ Minnesota Vikings

Green Bay Packers ★

Detroit Lions ★

New England Patriots ★

★ Buffalo Bills

Pittsburgh Steelers ★

Chicago Bears ★

Cleveland Browns ★

Philadelphia Eagles ★

★ New York Jets
★ New York Giants

Baltimore Ravens ★

Indianapolis Colts ★

★ Washington Commanders

★ Cincinnati Bengals

★ Kansas City Chiefs

★ Tennessee Titans

★ Carolina Panthers

★ Atlanta Falcons

★ Dallas Cowboys

★ Jacksonville Jaguars

New Orleans Saints ★

★ Tampa Bay Buccaneers

★ Houston Texans

★ Miami Dolphins

HOW TO USE THIS BOOK

Every team has two recipes: An appetizer to devour during kickoff and the first half of the game and a heartier entrée to demolish during halftime, intended to give you sustenance to weather the rest of the game.

Even though your team only has two recipes, you're not limited in what to cook from this book. Here are some ways to enjoy all the recipes:

- Make every game day special by cooking the recipes of the opposing team and literally bringing something new to the table each week.

- If your team has a bye week, then cook some of the team recipes for the game you're most excited to watch that week.

- If a recipe catches your fancy but has nothing to do with the game you're watching, go for it. There are no penalty flags thrown here!

- If you are part of a Fantasy Football league, have the members of the group make different recipes for meetups.

- You don't even have to make these recipes for a game day or anything related to football. Incorporate your favorites into daily meals and special occasions.

The options are truly endless!

TOUCHDOWN

Offense: Pantry Items

These are the basic ingredients you'll want to have on hand to make most of the recipes—and you probably already have most of them in your kitchen.

OILS, VINEGARS & SAUCES

Nonstick cooking spray

Olive oil

Vegetable oil

White vinegar

Apple cider vinegar

Soy sauce

Fish sauce

Worcestershire sauce

SEASONINGS, SPICES & DRIED HERBS

Table salt

Kosher salt

Seasoned salt

Black pepper

Italian seasoning

Old Bay seasoning

Dry mustard (aka ground mustard and mustard powder)

Paprika

Smoked paprika

Chili powder

Cayenne pepper

Ground cumin

Red pepper flakes

Bay leaves

Dried thyme

GRAINS & SEEDS

White rice

Pasta (spaghetti, penne, elbow macaroni)

All-purpose flour

Cornmeal

Italian bread crumbs

Panko bread crumbs

Sesame seeds

CANNED GOODS

Crushed tomatoes

Diced tomatoes

Tomato paste

Chicken broth/stock

Beef broth/stock

Vegetable broth/stock

SWEETENERS

Granulated sugar

Brown sugar

Honey

Maple syrup

CONDIMENTS

Ketchup

Yellow mustard

Dijon mustard

Extra-heavy mayonnaise

Hot sauce

Sriracha sauce

Barbecue sauce

Defense: Kitchen Tools

Besides pots, pans, baking sheets, knives, cutting boards, wooden spoons, spatulas, and everything else you most likely have in your cabinets and drawers, here are some tools that will help with the preparation of these recipes:

BLENDER OR IMMERSION BLENDER

SMALL FOOD PROCESSOR

SLOW COOKER

RICE COOKER

CAST-IRON SKILLET

(MEDIUM SIZE)

MICROPLANE/ ZESTER

MANDOLINE

(FOR THIN, EVEN SLICES)

GRATER BOX

(NO NEED TO BUY PRE-SHREDDED CHEESE)

CHARCOAL GRILL

TOOTHPICKS

(FOR SERVING AND SECURING)

SMOKER

(OPTIONAL)

Special Teams: Food Safety

A great tailgate or game-day party isn't just about the food; it's about keeping it safe so no one ends up taking a trip to the ER. When considering making these recipes for tailgating, be mindful that most stadium lots don't have refrigeration, running water, or kitchen facilities, so proper planning is key. When bringing food to another fan's house you can also follow these simple tips to keep your game-day eats fresh and safe.

HELPFUL TOOLS

HOT FOOD

- Insulated containers
- Thermal bags
- Towels
- Disposable aluminum pans/chafing trays
- Sterno cans
- Aluminum foil

COLD FOOD

- High-quality coolers
- Ice packs/frozen water bottles
- Ice
- Aluminum foil

SANITATION AND SERVING

- Hand sanitizer
- Disinfectant wipes
- Paper towels
- Extra utensils

KEEPING HOT FOOD HOT

- Hot dishes should be cooked at home and transported in insulated containers, slow cookers wrapped in towels, or thermal bags. The goal is to keep food at 135°F (57°C) or higher until it's time to eat. If it cools down at the tailgate, reheat it to 165°F (74°C) on a gas or charcoal grill. At another fan's home, use their oven or microwave.

- Disposable aluminum pans and chafing trays with Sterno cans are lifesavers for keeping things warm in the parking lot or at the party.

SANITATION AND SERVING

- Without fresh water readily available at a tailgate, hand sanitizer and disinfectant wipes are must-haves.

- No matter where you enjoy your food, bring/use extra utensils to avoid cross-contamination between raw and cooked foods.

- Perishables should never sit out for more than two hours—or one hour if it's over 90°F (32°C).

- Serve cold dips in bowls nestled in ice and keep grilled meats covered until eaten.

KEEPING COLD FOOD COLD

- Cold food must stay at 41°F (5°C) or below, but without a refrigerator, you must pack smart. Use high-quality coolers, layering ice packs or frozen water bottles around food. Keep raw meats in separate, sealed containers at the bottom of the cooler to avoid cross-contamination. Open the cooler only when necessary to maintain temperature.

- At a game-day party, keep cold foods in the fridge until ready to serve or over ice if placed on a buffet.

Remember, great game-day foods aren't just about flavor; it's about serving up food that keeps everyone safe for pregame, all four quarters, and beyond.

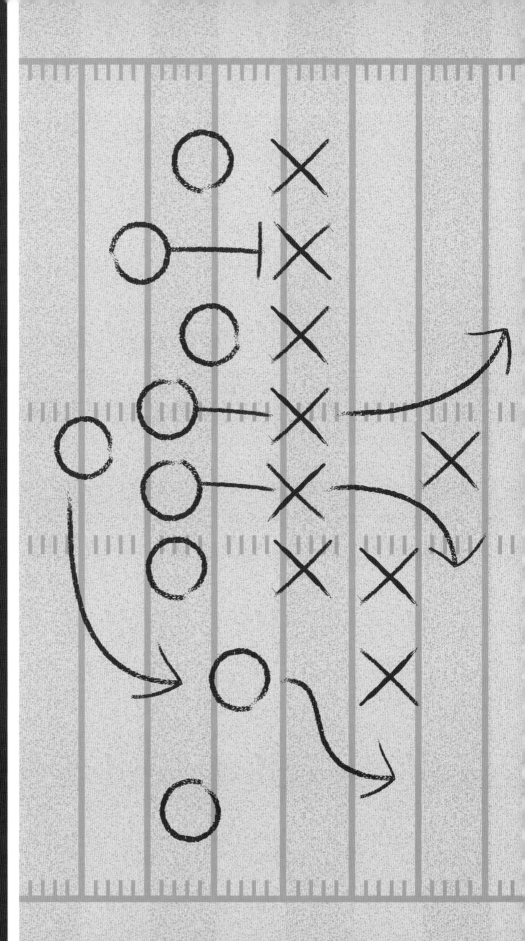

AFC

AFC NORTH

BALTIMORE RAVENS
CINCINNATI BENGALS
CLEVELAND BROWNS
PITTSBURGH STEELERS

AFC SOUTH

HOUSTON TEXANS
INDIANAPOLIS COLTS
JACKSONVILLE JAGUARS
TENNESSEE TITANS

AFC EAST

BUFFALO BILLS
MIAMI DOLPHINS
NEW ENGLAND PATRIOTS
NEW YORK JETS

AFC WEST

DENVER BRONCOS
KANSAS CITY CHIEFS
LAS VEGAS RAIDERS
LOS ANGELES CHARGERS

★ AFC ★ NORTH

BALTIMORE RAVENS

CRAB CAKE BITES 21

PIT BEEF SANDWICHES WITH HORSERADISH SAUCE 22

CINCINNATI BENGALS

HANKY PANKY 25

SKYLINE CHILI 26

CLEVELAND BROWNS

CITY "CHICKEN" BITES 29

POLISH BOY SANDWICHES 30

PITTSBURGH STEELERS

CHIPPED CHOP HAM SLIDERS 33

SEARED POLISH SAUSAGE AND PIEROGIES 34

Crab Cake Bites

PREP TIME: 10 minutes, plus 30 minutes chilling

COOK TIME: 15 minutes

YIELD: 14 to 16 bites

The history of crab cakes in the Baltimore region dates back to the early colonial era when settlers first began to explore the culinary potential of the local blue crab, a species abundant in the Chesapeake Bay. Numerous restaurants in Baltimore are renowned for their crab cakes, each offering a unique rendition of this classic dish. Faidley's Seafood, located in the historic Lexington Market, is perhaps the most famous, known for its award-winning crab cakes that attract locals and tourists alike.

CRAB CAKES

2 large eggs

½ cup (120 ml) heavy mayonnaise

¼ cup (60 ml) Dijon mustard

4 teaspoons Worcestershire sauce

4 teaspoons fresh lemon juice

4½ teaspoons Old Bay Seasoning

3 tablespoons minced fresh flat-leaf parsley

2 pounds (907 g) lump or jumbo lump crabmeat (use blue claw crabmeat for authentic Maryland cakes)

⅔ cup (55 g) panko bread crumbs

Nonstick cooking spray

2 tablespoons finely chopped chives

OLD BAY SAUCE

¾ cup (180 g) mayonnaise

3 teaspoons Dijon mustard

2 tablespoons olive oil

1 teaspoon hot sauce of choice

1 lemon, zested

1¼ teaspoons Old Bay Seasoning

¼ teaspoon granulated onion

¼ teaspoon ground black pepper

2 tablespoons minced fresh parsley

2 cloves garlic, minced

FOR SERVING

Lemon slices

Chopped chives

1 To make the crab cake bites: In an extra-large bowl, whisk together the eggs, ½ cup (120 ml) mayonnaise, ¼ cup (60 ml) mustard, Worcestershire sauce, lemon juice, 4½ teaspoons Old Bay, and 3 tablespoons parsley; make sure the eggs are thoroughly beaten.

2 Add the crabmeat 1 pound (454 g) at a time, slowly and gently mixing with a rubber spatula until all the crabmeat is coated. Add the panko, making sure not to break up the lumps of crabmeat while mixing; the mixture should stick together at the end of the spatula (see Two-Point Conversion).

3 Form the crab mixture into small balls using a 1-ounce (28 g) scoop and place onto a baking sheet greased with cooking spray about 1 inch (2.5 cm) apart (see Two-Point Conversion). Try not to handle them too much. Cover the crab cake bites with plastic wrap and refrigerate for at least 30 minutes, or up to 1 hour; this will help set the bread crumbs with the wet mixture and develop flavors.

4 Meanwhile, make the Old Bay sauce: In a medium bowl, whisk together the ¾ cup (180 g) mayonnaise, 3 teaspoons mustard, olive oil, hot sauce, grated lemon zest, 1¼ teaspoons Old Bay, onion, pepper, 2 tablespoons parsley, and garlic. Cover and refrigerate until needed.

5 Preheat the oven to 450°F (230°C). Bake the bites for 10 to 12 minutes, until golden brown and the internal temperature is at least 165°F (75°C). Let cool slightly and place on a serving tray. Garnish with the 2 tablespoons chopped chives.

6 Serve with the Old Bay sauce garnished with chives and some sliced lemon for squeezing.

TWO-POINT CONVERSION

If the crabmeat mixture isn't holding together, gradually add more bread crumbs until it comes together. Do not add more than 2 tablespoons of bread crumbs, as more than this will make the crab cakes dry.

If you do not have a 1-ounce (28 g) scoop, you can use two tablespoons to scoop and shape the cakes.

BALTIMORE RAVENS

Pit Beef Sandwiches with Horseradish Sauce

PREP TIME: 20 minutes, plus 2 hours 20 minutes marinating and resting

COOK TIME: 1 hour 30 minutes

YIELD: 4 to 6 sandwiches

PIT BEEF

4 to 5 pounds (1.8 to 2.3 kg) bottom round of beef

3 tablespoons seasoned salt

1 tablespoon granulated garlic

HORSERADISH SAUCE

¾ cup (180 ml) heavy mayonnaise

¼ cup (60 ml) sour cream

⅓ cup (80 g) prepared horseradish

Dash Worcestershire sauce

2 pinches salt

2 pinches black pepper

2 teaspoons dry mustard (aka ground mustard and mustard powder)

SANDWICHES

4 to 6 kaiser rolls

1 medium white onion, thinly sliced

Pit beef is a beloved regional specialty that traces its origins to the working-class neighborhoods of Baltimore. This iconic dish is essentially a charcoal-grilled beef sandwich, known for its distinctive smoky flavor and charred exterior. Different from barbecue-style beef, which is cooked low and slow, pit beef is cooked very quickly. The tradition of pit beef goes back to the 1970s, when it became popular at roadside stands and local taverns. Several restaurants in Baltimore are renowned for their pit beef offerings. Chaps Pit Beef is perhaps the most famous, having gained national attention for its hearty sandwiches.

1 To make the pit beef: Trim the beef then season it on all sides (see Two-Point Conversion) with the seasoned salt and garlic. Refrigerate the beef for up to 2 hours, or overnight for best results.

2 To make the horseradish sauce: In a medium bowl, mix the mayonnaise, sour cream, horseradish, Worcestershire sauce, salt, pepper, and dry mustard until well combined. Refrigerate while the beef is cooking.

3 Using a charcoal grill, start a fire on just one side of the grill (see Two-Point Conversion). When the coals have burned down with ash over them, put the beef on the grill over the hot coals. Turn the meat as it cooks, 6 to 7 minutes per side, until it has a dark char and color all over.

4 Move the meat to the side of the grill without the coals and cover. Let the meat roast, flipping once or twice, checking its internal temperature until it reaches about 120°F (50°C), about 1 hour and 30 minutes. Remove the meat from the grill and let rest for 20 minutes in a shallow pan before slicing thinly with a slicer knife. (Meat should always be sliced against the grain to get the thinnest, most tender slices.)

5 To assemble the sandwiches: Cut the kaiser rolls in half horizontally and place some sliced beef on the bottom halves. Top with horseradish sauce, slices of white onion, and the remaining halves of the rolls.

TWO-POINT CONVERSION

The bottom round of beef may have a silver skin not trimmed off by the butcher. Trim this off completely as it is inedible and if left on will leave a rubbery texture on the outside of the beef.

If you do not have a charcoal grill, simply prepare the raw meat as directed and sear on the stovetop in a cast-iron pan until browned deeply on all sides, then finish in an oven preheated to 350°F (180°C) for 1 hour and 45 minutes, or an internal temperature of 135°F (57°C). Let rest for for minutes before slicing and serving. The beauty of using cast iron is that it will create an even sear, and you can go right from the stovetop to the oven.

CINCINNATI BENGALS

Hanky Panky

PREP TIME: 10 minutes

COOK TIME: 15 minutes

YIELD: 36 servings

1 pound (454 g) ground spicy Italian pork sausage

1 pound (454 g) ground chuck beef (80/20)

2 cloves garlic, minced

1 tablespoon Worcestershire sauce

½ teaspoon paprika, plus more for garnishing

1 teaspoon dried oregano

1 teaspoon kosher salt

½ pound (227 g) Velveeta, diced medium

1 (12-ounce, or 340-g) package dark pumpernickel party bread or rye party bread

12 slices Velveeta cheese slices, each cut into 6 strips (72 strips total)

1 cup (50 g) roughly chopped fresh flat-leaf parsley, for garnishing

Hanky panky is a regional appetizer in Cincinnati, rooted in the city's rich tradition of comfort food. Often served at parties, family gatherings, and football games, hanky panky has become not only a local restaurant appetizer of some appeal, but also a time-tested family recipe passed down through generations. The basic recipe is a savory blend of ground beef, pork sausage, and a generous amount of Velveeta cheese. The mixture is seasoned with spices and sometimes a dash of Worcestershire sauce, then spread on small slices of rye bread or party pumpernickel bread and baked until bubbly and golden.

1 Preheat the oven broiler and line a rimmed baking sheet with parchment paper.

2 In a large skillet, cook the sausage, beef, and garlic over medium heat, breaking up the meat with a wooden spoon, until the meat is fully cooked and browned. Drain any fat. Add the Worcestershire sauce, paprika, oregano, and salt and mix thoroughly.

3 While the meat mixture is still hot in the pan, add the diced Velveeta, stirring until the cheese melts.

4 Spread the bread slices on the prepared baking sheet and place about 1 tablespoon of meat on each slice. Place 2 cheese strips in an X on top of the meat on each slice.

5 Place the pan in the oven and broil until the cheese melts, 20 to 35 seconds.

6 Serve hot on a large serving tray. Garnish with paprika and chopped parsley.

Skyline Chili

PREP TIME: 10 minutes

COOK TIME: 1 hour 30 minutes

YIELD: 6 to 8 servings

1 quart (960 ml) cold water

2 pounds (907 g) ground beef (80/20)

2 medium yellow onions, diced small

6 cloves garlic, minced

1 bay leaf

2 tablespoons apple cider vinegar

2 (8-ounce, or 227 g) cans tomato sauce

2 teaspoons Worcestershire sauce

2 teaspoons kosher salt

1 teaspoon ground cumin

½ teaspoon ground allspice

3 tablespoons dark chili powder

¼ teaspoon cayenne pepper

1 teaspoon ground cinnamon

2 tablespoons quality unsweetened cocoa powder (I use Hershey's)

Skyline Chili is an iconic regional dish that has become synonymous with Cincinnati. Founded in 1949 by Greek immigrant Nicholas Lambrinides, the Skyline Chili restaurant introduced a unique twist on traditional chili, blending Mediterranean spices with a hearty meat sauce. The dish is named after the view of the Cincinnati skyline from the restaurant's location atop Price Hill on the west side of the city. Skyline Chili is typically served over spaghetti or hot dogs, known as Coneys, and topped with shredded cheddar cheese, onions, and beans, creating the popular "three-way," "four-way," and "five-way" variations. The original restaurant still serves the dish to loyal customers, and many local diners and eateries also offer their take. The recipe below is for the chili only.

1 Put the water into a large saucepan. Break up the ground beef with your fingers into small chunks and stir into the water. Bring to a boil, then reduce the heat to medium and let simmer for 30 minutes. While the ground beef is cooking, use a small ladle or large kitchen spoon to skim the fat from the surface of the liquid and discard.

2 Add the onions, garlic, and bay leaf to the pot along with the vinegar, tomato sauce, and Worcestershire sauce. Mix thoroughly.

3 Add the salt, cumin, allspice, chili powder, cayenne pepper, cinnamon, and cocoa powder and mix to combine. Cook over medium heat for another hour, stirring occasionally.

4 Remove the bay leaf and serve the chili your favorite way (see Extra Point).

EXTRA POINT

Most people in Cincinnati order Skyline Chili as a "three-way," with the chili served over spaghetti and topped with a large amount of shredded cheddar. They use a knife and fork to cut the dish up, making it easier to eat and taste all the layers at once. If you plan to serve it this way, you will need 1 pound (454 g) of spaghetti, cooked, and 8 to 10 cups (0.9 to 1.2 kg) of shredded cheddar cheese to make the recommended servings. The chili is also usually served with oyster crackers and hot sauce.

CLEVELAND BROWNS

City "Chicken" Bites

PREP TIME: 30 minutes, plus 20 minutes chilling

COOK TIME: 40 minutes

YIELD: 12 bites

Nonstick cooking spray

1 teaspoon Lawry's Seasoned Salt

¼ teaspoon black pepper

¼ teaspoon dried thyme

¼ teaspoon paprika

2 (1½-pound, or 680-g) pork tenderloins, cut into 24 (1-inch, or 2.5-cm) cubes

1½ cups (190 g) all-purpose flour

4 large eggs

3 tablespoons whole milk

2 cups (200 g) Italian-seasoned bread crumbs

2 to 3 cups (480 to 720 ml) vegetable oil, for frying

1 cup (240 ml) low-sodium chicken stock

1 (12-ounce, or 340-g) jar pork or chicken gravy

½ cup (25 g) roughly chopped fresh flat-leaf parsley, for garnishing

City chicken is a beloved regional dish in Cleveland that can trace its roots to the early twentieth century, when chicken was a luxury and pork was more affordable. Despite its name, city chicken contains no chicken at all. It consists of cubed pork, or sometimes a combination of pork and veal, skewered to resemble a chicken leg, then it is breaded, pan-fried, and often baked or simmered in a broth until tender. City chicken remains a popular comfort food in Cleveland, often served at family gatherings and local diners that celebrate traditional Polish and Eastern European cuisine. This recipe is for an appetizer version of the dish and can be served with gravy on the side.

1 Preheat the oven to 350°F (175°C). Grease a large glass baking dish with nonstick spray.

2 In a small bowl, mix the seasoned salt, pepper, thyme, and paprika until well combined. Toss half of this mixture with the pork, making sure to fully coat the meat. Combine the remaining seasoning with the flour in a large bowl.

3 Set up a breading station with the bowl of seasoned flour, the eggs and milk whisked together in a separate large bowl, and the bread crumbs in a third bowl. Place a large platter next to the bread crumbs. Toss the seasoned pork cubes in the flour bowl, shaking off excess. Skewer 2 cubes onto a toothpick or short skewer, then dip into the egg mixture, followed by the bread crumbs. Repeat with the remaining pork. Arrange the pork skewers on the platter, making sure not to overlap them. Place the platter in the refrigerator to chill for up to 20 minutes to set the coating.

4 Heat the vegetable oil in a large pot over medium-high heat. (Test if the oil is hot enough by dropping in some bread crumbs and seeing if they sizzle and fry.) Carefully fry the pork skewers, in batches, for about 2 minutes on each side, or until the crust is set and golden brown. Drain on a paper towel–lined plate, then transfer to the prepared baking dish, leaving space between each skewer and making sure the skewers are lying down, not sticking up. Pour the chicken stock around the skewers and cover the dish tightly with foil.

5 Bake for 15 to 20 minutes, until the pork is tender and has reached an internal temperature of at least 145°F (63°C). Remove the foil and turn the oven to broil. Broil the skewers for 5 minutes to re-crisp them.

6 Meanwhile, heat the gravy to 165°F (75°C), then drizzle it over the skewers. Serve extra gravy in a small bowl on a platter, surrounded by the pork skewers. Garnish with the chopped parsley.

Polish Boy Sandwiches

PREP TIME: 20 minutes

COOK TIME: 20 minutes

YIELD: 8 sandwiches

The Polish boy embodies Cleveland's rich cultural diversity and love for hearty, flavorful food. This unique sandwich is believed to have originated in Cleveland's African American and Polish communities during the mid-twentieth century and consists of a grilled or fried kielbasa sausage placed in a bun and generously topped with layers of french fries, coleslaw, and tangy barbecue sauce. Local diners, food trucks, and barbecue joints throughout the city offer their own takes on this Cleveland classic, ensuring that the Polish boy remains a vibrant part of the city's culinary identity.

KIELBASA

4 (1-pound, or 454-g) smoked kielbasa rings, each ring cut into 2 pieces (8 sausages total)

1 tablespoon vegetable oil

SLAW

2 tablespoons yellow mustard

2 tablespoons mayonnaise

2 tablespoons apple cider vinegar

2 teaspoons Worcestershire sauce

1½ teaspoons kosher salt

2 teaspoons granulated sugar

½ teaspoon black pepper

½ teaspoon granulated garlic

1 (32-ounce, or 907-g) package coleslaw mix (shredded cabbage and carrots)

½ medium red onion, thinly sliced

SANDWICHES

8 (6-inch, or 15-cm) hoagie rolls, sliced horizontally and toasted

1 (26-ounce, or 737-g) bag frozen shoestring french fries

Favorite spicy barbecue sauce (I like Sweet Baby Ray's Chipotle BBQ)

1 **To make the kielbasa:** Lightly score (cut long, shallow slits into) the kielbasa skin with a sharp knife, then butterfly each sausage, being careful not to cut through the skin fully.

2 In a nonstick skillet, heat the vegetable oil over medium heat. Add the kielbasas, skin sides up, and cook, flipping over and searing until golden brown and sizzling, about 5 minutes per side. Remove from the pan and keep hot under foil.

3 **To make the slaw:** In a large bowl, whisk together the mustard, mayonnaise, vinegar, Worcestershire sauce, salt, sugar, pepper, and garlic. Add the slaw mix and red onion and toss until completely coated. Let the slaw sit for 5 to 10 minutes before serving.

4 Meanwhile, fry the french fries in a deep fryer or air fryer until crispy.

5 **To assemble the sandwiches:** Set a sausage in each toasted roll, skin side down. Top with the slaw and french fries. Drizzle with plenty of barbecue sauce and serve immediately.

PITTSBURGH STEELERS

Chipped Chop Ham Sliders

PREP TIME: 10 minutes

COOK TIME: 10 minutes

YIELD: 24 sliders

BARBECUE SAUCE

6 tablespoons white vinegar

¼ cup (60 ml) water

2 tablespoons sugar

¾ teaspoon dry mustard (aka ground mustard and mustard powder)

½ cup (120 ml) ketchup

1 teaspoon paprika

SANDWICHES

3 tablespoons butter

1½ pounds (68 g) deli "chopped ham," chipped on the meat slicer (ask at the deli counter; the ham should be very thin and almost shredded)

24 potato slider buns

FOR SERVING

Dill pickle spears, cut in half

The chipped chop ham sandwich is a quintessential Pittsburgh delicacy that reflects the city's industrial heritage and love for simple, satisfying foods. This sandwich is made with chipped chopped ham, a processed ham product that is shaved extremely thin, almost to the point of being shredded. The ham is typically seared and tossed with a sweet and tangy barbecue sauce and then piled high on a toasted soft sandwich bun. Isaly's Dairy Company began producing this budget-friendly meat product in the 1930s, and its affordability and unique texture quickly made it a staple in Pittsburgh households and delis. Isaly's still produces its famous chipped chopped ham, which is sold in grocery stores and featured in various local eateries. You can find this sandwich at long-standing Pittsburgh delis. The following recipe presents this classic as a slider, perfect as an appetizer for a crowd.

1 To make the barbecue sauce: In a small bowl, mix the vinegar, water, sugar, dry mustard, ketchup, and paprika until well combined.

2 To prepare the ham: Slice the butter into thin slices, then melt a few slices in a large nonstick pan over medium heat.

3 Add the chipped ham, in batches, to the pan, keeping an even layer and adding butter slices as needed. Sear the ham until golden brown, flipping over to sear the other side. Add some of the barbecue sauce to fully coat the ham, then let simmer for 5 minutes. Keep the ham warm.

4 If the buns are connected, slice them horizontally. Lightly toast the buns.

5 To assemble the sandwiches: Place the chipped ham on the bottom half of the buns, then top with the remaining bun halves. Secure each sandwich with a sandwich pick.

6 Immediately serve the sandwiches on a platter with dill pickle spears.

PITTSBURGH STEELERS

Seared Polish Sausage and Pierogies

PREP TIME: 20 minutes

COOK TIME: 30 minutes

YIELD: 6 servings

PIEROGIES

30 frozen cheese and potato pierogies (or any flavor you like; I also recommend onion and potato)

¼ cup (55 g, or ½ stick) butter

2 large yellow onions, diced small

⅛ teaspoon salt

MUSHROOM GRAVY

1 tablespoon vegetable oil

½ small onion, minced

2 slices cooked bacon, diced small

2 cloves garlic, minced

1½ cups (90 g) thinly sliced baby bella (cremini) mushrooms

¼ teaspoon kosher salt

1 teaspoon dried thyme

2 teaspoons fresh lemon juice

½ cup (120 ml) low-sodium chicken stock

½ cup (120 ml) heavy cream

⅛ teaspoon black pepper

1 tablespoon chopped fresh flat-leaf parsley

POLISH SAUSAGE

3 (1-pound, or 454-g) rings smoked Polish sausage (beef or pork kielbasa), each ring cut into 2 pieces (6 sausages total)

1 teaspoon vegetable oil

FOR GARNISHING AND SERVING

¼ cup (11 g) finely chopped chives

Sour cream

Pierogies are cherished in Pittsburgh, reflecting the city's rich Eastern European heritage. These dumplings, which originated in Poland and other Slavic countries, became a staple in Pittsburgh's kitchens as waves of immigrants brought their culinary traditions to the city in the late nineteenth and early twentieth centuries. In Pittsburgh, pierogies are widely available at local restaurants, delis, and community events. Pierogies even make appearances at Pittsburgh sporting events, with pierogi races held during Pirates baseball games. This recipe uses prepared pierogies and features a traditional Polish mushroom gravy, which complements the sausage in the dish.

1 Let the pierogies thaw while you are cooking the other ingredients.

2 Meanwhile, make the mushroom gravy: in a medium saucepan, heat the 1 tablespoon vegetable oil over medium-high heat. Add the minced onion and bacon and cook, stirring often, until the onion is translucent and the bacon is crisp.

3 Add the garlic, stirring often, until fragrant. Add the mushrooms, kosher salt, and thyme and cook, stirring occasionally, until all the moisture evaporates and the mushrooms turn dark golden brown.

4 Add the lemon juice to stop the cooking process, then add the stock. Bring to a simmer and let the liquid reduce by half. Add the heavy cream and reduce until the sauce thickens enough to coat the back of a spoon. Take the gravy off the heat and stir in the pepper and parsley. Keep warm.

5 To make the Polish sausage: Score (cut long, shallow slits into) the Polish sausages lightly with a sharp knife. In a large cast-iron skillet, heat the 1 teaspoon vegetable oil over medium heat for 2 minutes. Add the sausages, in batches, and sear until crispy and golden brown on all sides. Remove from the pan and keep warm under foil.

6 To make the pierogies: Melt the butter in a large nonstick skillet over medium-high heat. Add the pierogies, in batches, and sear them, being careful not to crowd the pan, until a slightly crispy golden-brown color on both sides, 2 to 3 minutes per side. Keep warm under foil. After the last batch of pierogies, add the diced onions and salt to the pan and cook, stirring often, until the onions are dark brown and fragrant.

7 Add the cooked pierogies back into the pan and toss with the caramelized onions and butter.

8 Serve 5 pierogies per plate with 1 piece of seared Polish sausage, all topped with mushroom gravy. Garnish with chives and serve with sour cream.

★ AFC ★ SOUTH

HOUSTON TEXANS

GREEN CHILI CHORIZO QUESO 39

BEEF BIRRIA TACOS 40

INDIANAPOLIS COLTS

FRIED BOLOGNA SANDWICHES 43

FRIED PORK TENDERLOIN SANDWICHES 44

JACKSONVILLE JAGUARS

MINI SALMON CROQUETTES WITH
REMOULADE SAUCE 47

STEAKS-IN-A-SACK 48

TENNESSEE TITANS

TENNESSEE WHISKEY PORK
BELLY BURNT ENDS 51

NASHVILLE HOT CHICKENS 52

HOUSTON TEXANS

Green Chili Chorizo Queso

PREP TIME: 15 minutes

COOK TIME: 20 minutes

YIELD: 20 servings

1 pound (454 g) ground chorizo sausage (or ground hot Italian sausage)

1 small onion, diced small

4 jalapeños, stem and seeds removed and diced small

3 poblano chili peppers, stem and seeds removed and diced small

3 cloves garlic, minced

2 or 3 vine-ripe tomatoes, diced small

1 (32-ounce, or 907-g) block Velveeta, diced into 1-inch (2.5 cm) cubes

1 cup (240 ml) half-and-half

2 tablespoons favorite hot sauce (I use Cholula)

½ tablespoon ground cumin

¼ cup (60 ml) fresh lime juice (about 2 limes)

1 cup (240 ml) water

Salt and black pepper

½ cup (20 g) chopped fresh cilantro

Tortilla chips, for serving

Green chili chorizo queso, known for its savory and spicy combination of melted cheese, roasted green chilies, and crumbled chorizo, is a popular dish in Houston's Tex-Mex cuisine. This rich dip draws on Mexican flavors while embracing the Tex-Mex tradition of queso, with the chorizo adding a bold, smoky element. The dish is usually served hot with tortilla chips, making it a perfect appetizer for sharing at social gatherings or before a hearty meal.

1 Brown the chorizo in a large cast-iron skillet over medium-high heat, breaking it up with a wooden spoon, for 5 to 7 minutes, until crispy. (Chorizo produces a lot of fat/grease when it is fully cooked, and the queso should never be greasy.) Drain the chorizo through a fine-mesh strainer or simply line a pasta strainer (colander) with paper towels and strain. Reserve 1 tablespoon of the fat. Keep the chorizo warm.

2 To the same skillet, add back the reserved chorizo fat, along with the onion, jalapeños, poblanos, and garlic, and cook, stirring often, over medium-high heat for 6 to 7 minutes, until the veggies start to brown.

3 Reduce the heat to low and add the drained chorizo back into the pan (see Extra Point). Combine with the peppers, onion, and garlic. Add the tomatoes, Velveeta, half-and-half, hot sauce, cumin, lime juice, and water, then stay with the skillet, stirring every few minutes until the cheese is fully melted and all ingredients are combined. If the queso is too thick, add a little more water (no more than ½ cup, or 120 ml) to thin it. Season with the salt and pepper to taste, then top the queso with the chopped cilantro.

4 Serve hot right from the skillet with tortilla chips for dipping.

EXTRA POINT

Some restaurants make this by topping the chili queso with the browned crispy chorizo, but you can also mix it in as I have done in this recipe. It all depends on whether you like your chorizo crispy on top or inside the queso.

PREP TIME: 25 minutes, plus overnight soaking

COOK TIME: 2 hours 30 minutes

YIELD: 30 servings

BEEF BIRRIA

5 dried ancho chili peppers

5 dried guajillo chili peppers

2 dried árbol chili peppers

4 pounds (1.8 kg) boneless chuck roast

Kosher salt

2 tablespoons vegetable oil, divided

1 medium yellow onion, diced medium

1 tablespoon tomato paste

6 cloves garlic, crushed

2½ quarts (10 cups, or 2.4 L) beef stock

1 cinnamon stick

6 bay leaves

1 tablespoon coriander seeds

1 tablespoon black peppercorns

6 sprigs fresh oregano

Salt and black pepper

TACOS

1 large Vidalia onion, finely chopped

1 cup (40 g) finely chopped fresh cilantro, divided

Juice of 1 lime

30 (6-inch, or 15-cm) corn tortillas

2 pounds (907 g) shredded Oaxaca cheese (or queso fresco or mozzarella)

Beef Birria Tacos

Beef birria tacos have become a favorite in Houston's vibrant food scene. The dish is rooted in traditional Mexican birria, a slow-cooked stew originating in Jalisco, Mexico. It's typically made with beef or goat, cooked in a blend of dried chilies, herbs, and spices until tender and flavorful. When served as tacos, the juicy meat is shredded, stuffed into corn tortillas, grilled to crispy perfection, and served with consommé for dipping.

1 To make the beef birria: Soak all the dried peppers in water overnight to soften. Slice the rehydrated chilies in half, then remove the stems and seeds. Preheat the oven to 350°F (175°C). Season the meat generously with the kosher salt.

2 Heat 1 tablespoon of the oil in a large Dutch oven over medium heat. Add the beef and sear for 3 to 4 minutes on all sides. Remove the meat from the pot and keep warm.

3 Reduce the heat to medium and add the remaining 1 tablespoon oil to the same pot. Add the yellow onion and cook, stirring often, until translucent. Add the tomato paste and cook, stirring frequently, until it begins to turn darker. Add the garlic and cook for 1 minute. Add the chilies and stock and mix well. Add the meat back into the pot.

4 Tie a piece of cheesecloth into a bag, enclosing the cinnamon stick, bay leaves, coriander, peppercorns, and oregano. Toss the bag into the pot and bring the liquid to a simmer. Cover the pot and carefully place it in the oven. Braise the beef for 1 hour.

5 While the beef is cooking, combine the Vidalia onion with ½ cup (20 g) of the chopped cilantro and the lime juice. Refrigerate.

6 After the meat has braised, carefully remove the pot from the oven. Remove the chilies and transfer them to a blender with a little of the cooking broth. Blend until smooth. Pour this mixture back into the pot and bring back to a simmer on the stovetop. Cover the pot, then carefully place it back into the oven and cook for 1 hour and 30 minutes, or until the meat is fork-tender and over 190°F (88°C). Remove the beef from the pot and shred it with a fork and tongs. Remove and discard the cheesecloth. Strain the broth. Taste it and season with salt and pepper. Keep hot.

7 To assemble the tacos: Heat a large, dry skillet over medium heat. Dunk 2 tortillas at a time in the strained broth (consommé) to cover completely. Place the tortillas in the skillet and top each one with shredded cheese and a little cilantro-onion-lime mixture. Add some shredded meat. When the tortillas are crisp, fold them over and remove from the skillet. Keep warm.

8 Serve on a large platter with a bowl of consommé in the middle for dipping. Top the tacos with the remaining ½ cup (20 g) cilantro.

INDIANAPOLIS COLTS

Fried Bologna Sandwiches

PREP TIME: 15 minutes

COOK TIME: 10 minutes

YIELD: 20 sandwich halves

10 thick slices bologna (¼ to ½ inch, or 6 to 12 mm, thick)

10 pats unsalted butter

10 slices yellow American cheese

20 slices plain white bread

Yellow mustard

2 medium yellow onions, thinly sliced into 10 slices total

2 medium tomatoes, sliced into 10 slices total

Shredded lettuce (optional)

Potato chips, for serving

The fried bologna sandwich is a nostalgic comfort food in Indianapolis, featuring thick-cut bologna slices fried to crispy perfection and served on soft white bread or a bun. Often topped with tomato, mustard, pickles, onions, and/or cheese, the sandwich offers a savory, salty bite that has long been a favorite in Indiana. It's a perfect representation of Midwestern cuisine, offering both simplicity and flavor, and is often served with chips or fries.

1 Heat a large skillet over medium-low heat. Cut 4 slits into the edges of each piece of bologna to prevent it from curling up.

2 Add 1 butter pat to the skillet and let it melt completely. Add 1 slice of bologna to the pan. Increase the heat to medium-high and sear the bologna for 1 to 2 minutes per side, until browned and slightly crispy. Transfer the slice to a large baking sheet and immediately top with 1 slice of cheese. Repeat with the remaining butter pats and bologna and cheese slices. Keep warm.

3 Lay out the 20 slices of bread, spreading mustard on every slice. Top 10 bread slices with 1 seared bologna slice with cheese, followed by 1 onion slice, 1 tomato slice, and shredded lettuce (if using). Close the sandwiches with the remaining bread slices.

4 Cut each sandwich in half. Serve the sandwiches on a large platter with potato chips.

EXTRA POINT

This sandwich can be prepared in different ways. Some recipes call for mayo instead of mustard; others add lettuce or even a fried egg. Make the sandwich to your taste. The important parts of the sandwich are the seared (fried) bologna and the use of white bread.

INDIANAPOLIS COLTS

Fried Pork Tenderloin Sandwiches

PREP TIME: 20 minutes, plus 20 minutes resting

COOK TIME: 30 minutes

YIELD: 10 sandwiches

10 center-cut pork loin chops (about ¾ inch, or 2 cm, thick), fat trimmed

8 cups (800 g) plain bread crumbs

2 teaspoons garlic powder

2 teaspoons salt, plus more to taste

1 teaspoon black pepper

3 cups (375 g) all-purpose flour

3 cups (720 ml) buttermilk

Vegetable oil

Kosher salt

10 leaves leaf lettuce

10 soft kaiser rolls, sliced in half horizontally

Yellow mustard

10 tomato slices

10 thin slices red onion

20 slices kosher pickles

Mayonnaise

French fries, for serving

The fried pork tenderloin sandwich is an iconic dish in Indianapolis, a true Midwestern favorite. This sandwich typically features pounded-thin pork tenderloin, breaded and deep-fried to crispy perfection. The tenderloin is often much larger than the bun it's served on. The sandwich is usually topped with lettuce, pickles, onions, and mustard or mayo, though variations exist. Originating in Indiana in the early twentieth century, it has become a symbol of Hoosier cuisine, drawing on the state's agricultural roots.

1 Butterfly each pork chop by cutting it horizontally but not completely through the other side. Lay open the chops. One at a time, cover each piece of pork with plastic wrap and, using the flat side of a meat mallet, pound until evenly flat and 6 to 8 inches (15 to 20 cm) wide.

2 Set up a breading station, with the bread crumbs, garlic powder, salt, and pepper mixed in a shallow dish until well combined; the flour in another shallow dish; and the buttermilk in a third one.

3 One at a time, dip both sides of a pork chop first into the flour and then into the buttermilk. Finally dip it into the bread crumbs and evenly coat on all sides. Place the breaded chops on a large dish, without letting them overlap, and let rest in the refrigerator for at least 20 minutes to set the crust.

4 Add at least 2 inches (5 cm) of oil to a large cast-iron skillet and heat to 375°F (190°C).

5 Carefully lower the breaded tenderloins into the hot oil, one at a time, and fry for about 2 minutes per side, or until fully golden brown and the internal temperature is at least 145°F (63°C). Place the fried pork chops on a cooling rack and sprinkle with salt. Keep warm.

6 To assemble the sandwiches, place 1 lettuce leaf on the bottom half of a roll. Squeeze mustard on top of the lettuce, followed by a fried pork chop, 1 tomato slice, 1 onion slice, and 2 pickle slices. Add the mayonnaise to the top halves of the rolls and close the sandwiches.

7 Serve these sandwiches on large plates, as the wide fried pork chop will hang off the roll on all sides, with french fries.

Mini Salmon Croquettes with Remoulade Sauce

PREP TIME: 15 minutes

COOK TIME: 10 minutes

YIELD: 20 croquettes

CROQUETTES

4 (14.75-ounce, or 418 g) cans pink salmon, drained and bones removed

2 teaspoons unsalted butter

1 cup (125 g) finely chopped yellow onion

1 cup (145 g) finely chopped green bell pepper

¾ cup (75 g) finely chopped celery

3 large eggs, beaten

2 teaspoons onion powder

2 teaspoons garlic powder

2 teaspoons black pepper

1 teaspoon salt

1 cup (125 g) all-purpose flour

Canola oil, for frying

REMOULADE SAUCE

1 cup (240 ml) mayonnaise

2 tablespoons Dijon mustard

2 teaspoons sweet pickle relish

1 tablespoon fresh lemon juice

1½ teaspoons minced fresh garlic

1 teaspoon black pepper

⅓ cup (15 g) minced chives

2 tablespoons finely chopped fresh flat-leaf parsley

2 tablespoons finely chopped fresh tarragon

Salmon croquettes are a beloved Southern dish, deeply rooted in African American culinary traditions, and have become a staple in Jacksonville. Made with canned or fresh salmon, onions, and seasonings, these croquettes are pan-fried to golden perfection. The dish originated as an affordable way to make canned fish more flavorful and has remained popular for its simplicity and comforting, savory taste. Serve these with sides of soul food classics like collard greens and corn bread for a hearty and flavorful meal.

1 **To make the croquettes:** In an extra-large bowl, break up the salmon into large flakes.

2 In a medium skillet, melt the butter over a medium-low heat. Add the onion, bell pepper, and celery and lightly cook, stirring often, until golden brown. Remove from the heat and let cool completely.

3 **Meanwhile, make the remoulade sauce:** Add all the sauce ingredients to a medium bowl and mix until well combined. Refrigerate until ready to serve.

4 Add the cooked onion, celery, and bell pepper to a large bowl along with the eggs, onion powder, garlic powder, 2 teaspoons black pepper, and salt. Gradually stir in the flour until completely mixed. Add the salmon, in batches, and mix gently so as not to break up the large flakes; make sure everything is thoroughly combined.

5 Shape the salmon mixture into 20 round patties, about 2 ounces 57 g) each (you can use a 2-ounce (57 g) scoop for this).

6 Heat a large skillet over medium heat. Add enough canola oil to coat the bottom of the pan. Once the oil is hot, carefully place 4 to 6 croquettes at a time in the pan and cook for about 3 minutes per side, or until golden brown and cooked through. Remove the patties from the pan and place them on a large paper towel–lined tray.

7 Serve hot on a large platter with the remoulade sauce for dipping.

JACKSONVILLE JAGUARS

Steak in a Sack

PREP TIME: 30 minutes, plus 30 minutes marinating

COOK TIME: 20 minutes

YIELD: 6 sandwiches

Simple and savory, the steak in a sack is a cherished regional favorite in Jacksonville. It typically features thinly sliced, grilled steak stuffed into a warm pita, often accompanied by lettuce, tomatoes, onions, and a tangy sauce. The dish is a fusion of Mediterranean and American culinary traditions, with influences from Jacksonville's Middle Eastern community. A well-known spot to find steak in a sack in Jacksonville is The Sheik Sandwiches and Subs, which has been serving this sandwich for decades as part of its traditional menu of Mediterranean American fusion.

STEAK IN A SACK

1½ teaspoons garlic powder

1½ teaspoons onion powder

1½ teaspoons paprika

⅔ teaspoon ground cumin

⅓ teaspoon black pepper

⅔ teaspoon salt

1½ pounds (680 g) sirloin steak, thinly sliced (about ⅛ inch, or 3 mm, thick)

1½ tablespoons vegetable oil

1 large yellow onion, thinly sliced

3 large pocket pita breads

6 slices deli-cut provolone cheese

SAUCE

¼ cup (60 ml) mayonnaise

2 tablespoons tahini

1 tablespoon fresh lemon juice

Pinch ground cumin

Pinch cayenne pepper

Pinch kosher salt

FOR SERVING

3 cups (165 g) shredded lettuce

2 large tomatoes, cut into wedges

French fries or potato chips

1 **To make the steak in a sack:** In a large bowl, mix the garlic powder, onion powder, paprika, cumin, black pepper, and salt until well combined. Add the steak slices and toss to coat evenly with the seasoning. Let marinate in the refrigerator for 30 minutes.

2 Heat the vegetable oil in a large skillet over medium-high heat. Cook the marinated steak, in batches, for 1 to 2 minutes per side, until browned, making sure each piece can lie flat without being overcrowded in the pan for an even sear. Remove from the pan and keep warm.

3 To the same pan, add the onion and cook, stirring often, for about 6 minutes, or until softened and browned.

4 **While the onions are cooking, make the sauce:** In a small bowl, mix the mayonnaise, tahini, lemon juice, cumin, cayenne pepper, and salt until smooth. Adjust seasoning to taste.

5 Add the cooked steak slices back into the pan with the onions and mix thoroughly.

6 **To assemble the steak in a sack:** Cut each pita in half, opening the pockets. Evenly spread 1 tablespoon of sauce in each pita. Add 1 slice of cheese, then add the steak and onion mixture.

7 Serve the sandwiches warm with the shredded lettuce, tomato wedges, and french fries or potato chips.

Tennessee Whiskey Pork Belly Burnt Ends

PREP TIME: 15 minutes

COOK TIME: 3 hours

YIELD: 12 servings

Tennessee whiskey–based barbecue is a Nashville favorite that blends the region's rich barbecue traditions with the distinct flavor of the state's famous whiskey. The whiskey glaze highlights the state's distilling heritage, particularly from nearby Lynchburg, home of Jack Daniel's. This recipe offers two methods for making pork belly burnt ends: a charcoal-grill method and a method cooked entirely in the oven.

BURNT ENDS

2 tablespoons paprika

2 tablespoons brown sugar

1 tablespoon garlic powder

1 tablespoon onion powder

2 teaspoons black pepper

1 teaspoon salt

4 pounds (1.8 kg) pork belly, cut into 1-inch (2.5 cm) cubes

2 tablespoons vegetable oil

GLAZE

½ cup (120 ml) Tennessee whiskey

¼ cup (60 ml) maple syrup

¼ cup (55 g) brown sugar

½ cup (120 ml) favorite barbecue sauce

2 tablespoons unsalted butter

1 tablespoon Dijon mustard

1 tablespoon apple cider vinegar

FOR SERVING

Favorite barbecue sauce (I like Sweet Baby Ray's Honey Barbecue Sauce)

1   **To make the burnt ends:** If using the charcoal-grill method, preheat the charcoal grill for indirect cooking by piling the lit charcoal on one side of the grill, leaving the other side empty. Adjust the vents to maintain a temperature of around 250°F (120°C). Soak wood chips or chunks (I use hickory) for 30 minutes in water. Once ready to cook, scatter the wood over the lit charcoal to create smoke. If using the oven method, preheat the oven to 250°F (120°C).

2   In a small bowl, mix the paprika, 2 tablespoons brown sugar, garlic powder, onion powder, pepper, and salt until well combined. In a large bowl, toss the pork belly cubes with the vegetable oil, then rub them with the seasoning mixture.

3   If using the charcoal-grill method, place the meat on aluminum foil on the side of the grill without direct heat. Cover the grill, ensuring the vent is over the pork belly to draw the smoke across the meat. Cook for 2 hours, maintaining the temperature at around 250°F (120°C), or until the cubes are crispy on the outside and tender on the inside. Check occasionally and add charcoal and/or wood chips if needed. If using the oven method, arrange the pork belly cubes on foil on a wire rack placed over a rimmed baking sheet; this will allow the fat to render and the meat to crisp. Roast the pork belly in the oven for 2 hours, or until the cubes are crispy on the outside and tender on the inside.

4   **Meanwhile, make the glaze:** Combine the whiskey, maple syrup, ¼ cup (55 g) brown sugar, barbecue sauce, butter, mustard, and vinegar in a medium saucepan. Simmer over medium-high heat for 5 to 7 minutes, stirring often, until the glaze thickens. Remove from the heat.

5   Transfer the crispy pork belly cubes to an aluminum foil pan. Pour the glaze over them, tossing to coat, then spread the cubes in an even layer. If using the grill, cover the pan with foil and place it on the grill (on the indirect heat side). If using the oven, increase the temperature to 275°F (135°C). Cover the pan with foil and place it in the oven. For both methods, cook for 45 minutes to 1 hour, until the glaze is caramelized. Let the pork belly rest for 10 minutes before serving.

6   Serve the burnt ends as an appetizer with toothpicks and barbecue sauce for dipping.

Nashville Hot Chicken

PREP TIME: 30 minutes, plus 1 hour marinating

COOK TIME: 1 hour

YIELD: 16 servings

Nashville hot chicken is a fiery regional specialty that has become synonymous with the city's food culture. The dish originated in the 1930s at Prince's Hot Chicken Shack where, legend has it, the fiery flavor was created as a revenge dish by a scorned lover. Instead of a punishment, the intensely spiced fried chicken became a favorite, and the recipe was passed down through generations. Nashville hot chicken is made by deep-frying chicken then coating it in a spicy paste made from cayenne pepper and other seasonings, delivering a signature heat that ranges from mild to mouth-blistering. It is served with classic sides like pickles, white bread, and coleslaw to balance the heat.

CHICKEN

5⅓ cups (1.3 L) buttermilk

3 tablespoons favorite hot sauce (I like Crystal)

8 bone-in, skin-on chicken thighs

8 bone-in, skin-on chicken drumsticks

5⅓ cups (690 g) all-purpose flour

2⅔ teaspoons salt

2⅔ teaspoons black pepper

1⅓ teaspoons paprika

1⅓ teaspoons garlic powder

1⅓ teaspoons onion powder

1⅓ teaspoons cayenne pepper

Vegetable oil, for frying

HOT SAUCE

1⅓ cups (260 g) cayenne pepper

⅓ cup (75 g) brown sugar

2⅔ tablespoons paprika

2⅔ tablespoons chili powder

2⅔ teaspoons garlic powder

2⅔ teaspoons salt

1⅓ teaspoons black pepper

FOR SERVING

16 slices plain white bread

Sweet dill pickles

1 To make the chicken: In a large bowl, mix the buttermilk and hot sauce. Add the chicken, ensuring all pieces are submerged and let marinate in the refrigerator for at least 1 hour, or overnight for more flavor.

2 In a separate bowl, mix the flour, salt, 2⅔ teaspoons black pepper, 1⅓ teaspoons paprika, 1⅓ teaspoons garlic powder, onion powder, and cayenne pepper until well combined.

3 Heat 1 to 2 inches (2.5 to 5 cm) of vegetable oil in a deep, heavy-bottom pot to 350°F (175°C). Remove the chicken from the marinade, discarding the marinade, and dredge each piece in the seasoned flour, coating the pieces well. Shake off excess flour.

4 Carefully fry 4 or 5 pieces of chicken at a time, being careful not to overcrowd the pot, for 12 to 15 minutes, flipping halfway through, until golden brown and the internal temperature reaches 165°F (75°C). Transfer to a paper towel–lined plate. Reserve 2 cups (480 ml) of the frying oil for the hot sauce, straining any pieces and/or flour out.

5 To make the hot sauce: In a metal bowl, whisk together the cayenne pepper, brown sugar, 2⅔ tablespoons paprika, chili powder, 2⅔ tablespoons garlic powder, salt, and 1⅓ teaspoons black pepper. Carefully whisk in the reserved hot frying oil until the sauce is smooth and well combined. Dip the chicken into the sauce, in batches, coating completely. (This sauce needs to be whisked back together each time before dipping the chicken into it, as the seasonings will settle at the bottom). Allow the chicken to drain over the sauce before transferring to individual serving plates.

6 Serve each chicken piece with white bread and pickles.

EXTRA POINT

You can add a side of store-bought coleslaw to balance the heat as you eat.

★ AFC ★ EAST

BUFFALO BILLS

BUFFALO CHICKEN DIP 57

ROAST BEEF ON WECK SANDWICHES 58

MIAMI DOLPHINS

AREPAS CON CHICHARRONES 61

CUBAN SANDWICHES 62

NEW ENGLAND PATRIOTS

FRIED CLAMS 65

LOBSTER ROLLS 66

NEW YORK JETS

PORK ROLL, EGG, AND CHEESE SANDWICHES 69

ITALIAN SAUSAGE AND PEPPERS SANDWICHES 70

BUFFALO
BILLS

Buffalo Chicken Dip

PREP TIME: 20 minutes

COOK TIME: 45 minutes

YIELD: 15 servings

1 tablespoon olive oil

1 tablespoon plus 2 teaspoons garlic powder, divided

1 tablespoon plus 2 teaspoons onion powder, divided

1 teaspoon paprika

1 teaspoon salt

½ teaspoon black pepper

2 pounds (907 g) boneless, skinless chicken breasts (about 4 large breasts)

16 ounces (454 g) cream cheese, softened

1½ cups (360 ml) Buffalo sauce (such as Frank's RedHot)

1 cup (240 ml) ranch dressing

1 cup (240 ml) blue cheese dressing (optional, or substitute with more ranch)

3 cups (345 g) shredded cheddar cheese, divided

1 cup (110 g) shredded mozzarella cheese

Nonstick cooking spray

Sliced scallions or chives, for garnishing

Tortilla chips and/or crackers, for serving

Carrot and/or celery sticks, for serving

Buffalo chicken dip is a beloved dish that evolved from Buffalo's iconic Buffalo wings, which originated at the Anchor Bar in the 1960s. The dip captures the wings' signature flavors by combining shredded chicken, hot sauce, and creamy elements like ranch or blue cheese dressing, along with melted cheeses. Often served warm, it's a popular choice for parties and game days, offering a crowd-pleasing mix of spicy, tangy, and creamy textures. The dish is typically enjoyed with tortilla chips and/or celery sticks, like how wings are served.

1 Preheat the oven to 375°F (190°C).

2 In a large bowl, mix the olive oil, 2 teaspoons of the garlic powder, 2 teaspoons of the onion powder, the paprika, salt, and pepper until well combined. Add the chicken breasts and evenly rub the seasonings all over them. Place the seasoned chicken on a rimmed baking sheet.

3 Bake for 20 to 25 minutes, until the internal temperature reaches 165°F (75°C). Let the chicken rest for 5 minutes before shredding with two forks or with the paddle in a stand mixer. Reduce the oven temperature to 350°F (175°C).

4 In a clean large bowl, combine the shredded chicken, cream cheese, Buffalo sauce, ranch dressing, and blue cheese dressing (if using). Stir in 2 cups (230 g) of the cheddar cheese, the mozzarella cheese, remaining 1 tablespoon garlic powder, and remaining 1 tablespoon onion powder. Mix until all the ingredients are fully combined.

5 Grease a 9 x 13-inch (23 x 33 cm) baking dish with nonstick spray. Transfer the chicken mixture to the prepared dish, spreading it evenly. Sprinkle the remaining 1 cup (115 g) cheddar cheese over the top.

6 Bake for 20 to 25 minutes, until bubbly and the cheese on top are melted and golden brown. Let the dip cool for a few minutes, then garnish with sliced scallions or chives.

7 Serve warm in the baking dish along with tortilla chips and/or crackers and carrot and/or celery sticks for dipping.

BUFFALO
BILLS

Roast Beef on Weck Sandwiches

PREP TIME: 20 minutes

COOK TIME: 1 hour
45 minutes

YIELD: 12 sandwiches

ROAST BEEF

2 tablespoons olive oil

1 tablespoon kosher salt

1 teaspoon black pepper

2 teaspoons garlic powder

1 teaspoon onion powder

1 teaspoon paprika

4 pounds (1.8 kg) beef top round or a sirloin roast

1 cup (240 ml) beef broth

HORSERADISH SPREAD

1 cup (215 g) prepared horseradish

½ cup (120 ml) mayonnaise

1 tablespoon Dijon mustard

1 teaspoon fresh lemon juice

Salt and black pepper

KUMMELWECK-STYLE ROLLS

12 kaiser rolls

2 tablespoons water

1 tablespoon coarse sea salt

1 tablespoon caraway seeds

FOR SERVING

12 cups (2.8 L) warm beef broth

12 dill or bread-and-butter pickle slices

Roast beef on weck is a beloved combination of tender roast beef served on a kummelweck roll. The kummelweck, a kaiser-style roll topped with coarse salt and caraway seeds, gives the sandwich its distinctive name and flavor. The sandwich is often served with a side of horseradish and au jus, perfect for dipping. The salty, crunchy roll contrasts beautifully with the juicy, thinly sliced roast beef, making it a staple of Buffalo's culinary scene. Two popular places to enjoy this classic are Charlie the Butcher, which has been serving this iconic sandwich since 1914, and Schwabl's, a historic Buffalo-area restaurant dating back to 1837. Both institutions are known for their authentic preparation of this sandwich, often accompanied by traditional sides like dill pickles and fries.

1 To make the roast beef: Preheat the oven to 325°F (165°C). In a small bowl, mix the olive oil, kosher salt, 1 teaspoon pepper, garlic powder, onion powder, and paprika until well combined. Rub the roast all over with the mixture. Place the roast in a roasting pan and add the broth to the pan.

2 Bake for 1 hour and 30 minutes to 2 hours, until the internal temperature reaches 135°F (57°C) for medium rare or 145°F (63°C) for medium. Let the roast rest for 15 minutes before thinly slicing. Reserve the beef broth for serving. Increase the oven temperature to 350°F (175°C).

3 Meanwhile, make the horseradish sauce: In a small bowl, mix the horseradish, mayonnaise, mustard, lemon juice, and salt and pepper to taste until well combined. Adjust the seasoning if necessary and set aside at room temperature.

4 To make the kummelweck-style rolls: Brush the tops of the kaiser rolls with water and sprinkle with the coarse sea salt and caraway seeds. Place the rolls on a baking sheet and bake for 5 to 7 minutes, until the tops are slightly crisp. Keep warm.

5 To assemble the sandwiches: Slice each "weck" roll in half horizontally and spread a layer of the horseradish sauce on the bottom halves. Top with a generous portion (about 5 ounces, or 142 g) of roast beef and close with the remaining roll halves. Serve each sandwich with 1 cup (240 ml) of warm beef broth for dipping and dill pickles.

EXTRA POINT

Serve with French fries or potato salad for a complete meal.

Arepas con Chicharrones

PREP TIME: 30 minutes

COOK TIME: 40 minutes

YIELD: 16 arepas

AREPAS

4 cups (720 g) masarepa (precooked cornmeal; see Extra Point)

2 teaspoons salt, plus more to taste

5 cups (1.2 L) warm water

2 tablespoons unsalted butter, melted

All-purpose flour, for dusting

3 tablespoons vegetable oil

CHICHARRONES

2 teaspoons salt, plus more to taste

2 pounds (907 g) skin-on pork belly, cut into 1-inch (2.5 cm) pieces

1 cup (240 ml) water

1 tablespoon baking soda

1 teaspoon garlic powder

1 teaspoon ground cumin

1 teaspoon black pepper

FOR SERVING

Lime wedges

Avocado slices

Chopped fresh cilantro

Favorite salsa

Arepas con chicharrones is a beloved dish in Miami, showcasing the city's rich cultural heritage, particularly its Venezuelan and Colombian influences. Arepas, which are made from precooked cornmeal, serve as a versatile base for various fillings. When paired with crispy chicharrones—fried pork belly seasoned to perfection—this dish delivers a delightful contrast of textures and flavors. The origins of arepas can be traced back to Indigenous cultures in Venezuela and Colombia, where corn was a staple food. In Miami, arepas con chicharrones can be found at several popular eateries.

1. **To make the arepas:** In a large bowl, combine the masarepa, salt, and warm water, stirring until it forms a dough. Add the melted butter and knead the dough in the bowl until it is smooth and free of lumps.

2. Place the dough on a lightly floured surface and divide it into 16 equal portions. Shape each portion into a ball with your hands, then flatten each ball into a disc about ½ inch (13 mm) thick.

3. Heat the vegetable oil in a large skillet over medium heat. Cook the arepas, in batches, for 5 to 7 minutes per side, until golden brown and crispy. Transfer to a paper towel–lined platter and keep warm.

4. **To make the chicharrones:** Season the pork belly cubes with the 2 teaspoons salt. Place the cubes in a large saucepan, add the water and baking soda, and bring to a boil over medium-high heat. Allow the pork to cook until the water evaporates and the fat begins to render, 15 to 20 minutes. Continue cooking the pork belly for 20 to 30 minutes, until it is golden brown and slightly crunchy on the outside and tender on the inside. After the pork is crispy, season with garlic powder, cumin, pepper, and more salt.

5. **To assemble the arepas:** On a large platter, arrange the arepas without overlapping them. Top each one with a portion of crispy chicharrones. Arrange lime wedges for squeezing and avocado slices and chopped cilantro for topping on the platter and serve with the salsa. To eat, fold the arepas in half around the fillings, like a sandwich.

EXTRA POINT

You can find masarepa in Latin American markets or in the supermarket in the Latin foods section. Two good brands to use are Goya and Pan.

MIAMI DOLPHINS

Cuban Sandwiches

PREP TIME: 15 minutes

COOK TIME: 15 minutes

YIELD: 12 sandwiches

12 Cuban bread rolls (or sub rolls)

½ cup (120 ml) yellow mustard

2 pounds (907 g) roasted pork, sliced thin (use sliced roast pork from a deli or see Extra Point)

1 pound (454 g) deli-sliced Black Forest or honey ham

1 pound (454 g) deli-sliced Swiss cheese

1 cup (110 g) sliced dill pickles

¼ cup (55 g, or ½ stick) unsalted butter, softened

Plantain chips, for serving (optional)

The Cuban is a quintessential sandwich that reflects Miami's rich cultural heritage, especially the city's strong Cuban community. This iconic sandwich is made with layers of succulent roast pork, sweet ham, Swiss cheese, pickles, and mustard, all pressed between slices of Cuban bread. The origins of the Cuban sandwich can be traced back to the late nineteenth century, when Cuban immigrants in Florida began blending their culinary traditions with local ingredients. Versailles in Miami, known as the "most famous Cuban restaurant in the world," offers an authentic Cuban sandwich that attracts both locals and tourists alike. Typically, the sandwich is accompanied by plantain chips or a refreshing side salad.

1   Preheat a griddle or large skillet over medium heat. If using a panini press, preheat it according to the manufacturer's instructions.

2   Slice the Cuban bread rolls in half horizontally. Spread yellow mustard on the inside of both the top and bottom halves. Layer each bottom roll with roasted pork, followed by ham, cheese, and pickles. Top with the remaining roll halves, then spread a thin layer of softened butter on the outside of both the top and bottom halves of each roll; this will help create a crispy crust during cooking.

3   Place the sandwiches on the preheated griddle or skillet. If using a panini press, place the sandwiches inside and close it. Cook for 3 to 5 minutes per side, until the bread is golden brown and crispy and the cheese is melted. If using a griddle or skillet, press down on the sandwiches with a spatula or a heavy pan to compress them while cooking.

4   Remove the sandwiches from the heat, slice them diagonally, and serve immediately with plantain chips (if using).

EXTRA POINT

If you want to make this sandwich traditional, with authentic flavor, find a recipe online to make pernil (Cuban roast pork).

NEW ENGLAND PATRIOTS

Fried Clams

PREP TIME: 30 minutes

COOK TIME: 10 minutes

YIELD: 15 servings

2 pounds (907 g) fresh-shucked whole belly clams (or use three 10-ounce, or 283-g, cans of whole baby clams, drained and rinsed; see Extra Point)

2 cups (200 g) prepared seasoned fish fry mix (I like House Autry or Louisiana; make sure it is seasoned but not Cajun- or creole-spiced)

1 cup (240 ml) buttermilk (or substitute with half-and-half)

Vegetable oil, for frying

Salt and black pepper

Lemon wedges, for serving

Tartar or cocktail sauce, for serving

Fried clams are a quintessential New England dish that dates to the early twentieth century, when they were popularized by the clam shacks that dotted the coastline. The dish typically features fresh, sweet clams that are lightly breaded and fried until golden brown, creating a crispy exterior that perfectly complements the tender, succulent meat inside. This beloved seafood dish often evokes nostalgic memories of summer visits to the beach, where diners would indulge in the simple pleasure of fried clams served with lemon wedges and dipping sauces.

1 If using fresh-shucked whole belly clams, rinse them under cold water to remove any sand or grit. (For canned clams, make sure they are drained fully.) Pat the clams dry with paper towels.

2 Set up a breading station with the fish fry mix in a shallow dish and the buttermilk in another.

3 Dip each clam into the buttermilk, allowing any excess to drip off, then dredge in the fish fry mix, ensuring it is evenly coated. Place the breaded clams on a large platter in an even layer, making sure not to overlap them. Place the clams in the refrigerator for 10 minutes while heating the oil.

4 In a large, heavy-bottomed pot, heat about 2 inches (5 cm) of oil over medium-high heat until it reaches 350°F (175°C). (You can test the oil by dropping a small amount of the buttermilk–fish fry mixture into it; it should sizzle and float to the top.)

5 Remove the clams from the refrigerator. Carefully add the breaded clams, in batches, to the hot oil and fry for 2 to 3 minutes, until golden brown and crispy on both sides. Transfer the clams to a paper towel–lined plate. Season with salt and pepper to taste.

6 Serve the fried clams hot on a large platter with lemon wedges for squeezing and tartar or cocktail sauce for dipping.

EXTRA POINT

You can also cut the clams into strips if you prefer fried clam strips.

NEW ENGLAND PATRIOTS

Lobster Rolls

PREP TIME: 30 minutes

COOK TIME: 10 minutes

YIELD: 12 rolls

LOBSTER FILLING

3 pounds (1.4 kg) cooked lobster meat, chopped (6 to 8 lobsters' worth; you can buy this frozen or cook your own lobsters and clean)

MAYO VERSION

½ cup (120 ml) mayonnaise

2 tablespoons fresh lemon juice

1 teaspoon kosher salt, or to taste

½ teaspoon black pepper, or to taste

½ cup (50 g) minced celery

¼ cup (11 g) minced chives

BUTTER VERSION

½ cup (115 g) clarified butter

2 tablespoons fresh lemon juice

1 teaspoon kosher salt, or to taste

½ teaspoon black pepper, or to taste

BUNS

3 tablespoons unsalted butter

12 split-top New England-style hot dog buns

FOR GARNISHING AND SERVING

Finely chopped fresh flat-leaf parsley

Potato chips

Coleslaw (optional)

Lobster rolls typically feature fresh, sweet lobster meat, which can be served either tossed in mayonnaise or mixed with clarified butter. The choice between these two preparations often sparks passionate debate among New Englanders and seafood enthusiasts. While the mayonnaise version is creamy and cool, the buttered version highlights the rich, savory flavor of the lobster, creating a decadent experience. The origins of the lobster roll can be traced back to the early 1900s, but the dish gained popularity in the 1920s and '30s as seafood shacks began serving it as a quick, satisfying meal.

1 To prepare the lobster filling: If using frozen lobster meat, make sure it is completely thawed, drained, and patted dry with paper towels. If using fresh, make sure it is drained and patted dry with paper towels.

2 **A** To make the mayo version: To a large bowl, add the chopped lobster meat, mayonnaise, lemon juice, salt, pepper, celery, and chives, mixing gently to combine. Taste and adjust the seasoning if necessary.
B To make the butter version: To a large bowl, add the chopped lobster meat with the clarified butter, lemon juice, salt, and pepper, tossing gently until the lobster is well coated. Taste and adjust the seasoning if necessary.

3 To prepare the buns: Heat a large skillet over medium heat. Add the unsalted butter and allow it to fully melt. Place the split buns in the skillet, cut sides down, and toast until golden brown, 2 to 3 minutes.

4 For each lobster roll, spoon a generous portion of the lobster filling (4 ounces, or 113 g) into a toasted bun. Garnish with the chopped parsley. Serve the lobster rolls immediately with potato chips and/or coleslaw (if using).

EXTRA POINT

If you want to make both butter and mayo versions, use 1½ pounds (680 g) of lobster for each version and halve the other ingredients.

NEW YORK JETS

Pork Roll, Egg, and Cheese Sandwiches

PREP TIME: 20 minutes

COOK TIME: 15 minutes

YIELD: 24 sandwich halves

12 New York hard rolls or kaiser rolls, sliced in half horizontally

1 (12-ounce, or 340-g) pork roll, sliced into 24 rounds (about ¼ inch, or 6 mm, thick)

2 tablespoons unsalted butter

12 large eggs

Salt and black pepper

12 deli slices American cheese

Ketchup and/or favorite hot sauce, for serving

Pork roll, egg, and cheese on a hard roll is a quintessential breakfast sandwich in New Jersey. The sandwich features crispy seared pork roll (Taylor ham), a fried egg, and melted American cheese, served on a firm hard roll or kaiser roll. A regional debate rages over the meat's name: Residents from North Jersey call it Taylor ham—named after the 1856 creation by John Taylor—and South Jersey residents refer to it as pork roll, the more generic name applied after regulations required non-ham products to drop the "ham" label.

1 Preheat the oven to 350°F (175°C). Place the rolls on two separate parchment-lined baking sheets, so each roll lies flat, open like a book.

2 Make 3 small slits around the edges of each pork roll slice to prevent curling during cooking. In a large nonstick skillet over medium-high heat, cook the pork roll slices, in batches, for 2 to 3 minutes per side, until browned and crispy. Remove from the skillet and keep warm.

3 Melt the butter in the same skillet over medium heat. Crack the eggs into the skillet, cooking, in batches, to just past over-medium, allowing the yolks to remain slightly runny. (If a fully cooked yolk is preferred, cook the eggs until the yolks are fully set.) Season with salt and pepper to taste.

4 Place 1 slice of cheese on each roll half. Bake the rolls for 3 to 5 minutes, until the cheese is melted. Turn off the oven, keeping the open rolls warm in it.

5 To assemble the sandwiches, layer 2 pork roll slices on top of the melted cheese on each bottom roll, then top with 1 cooked egg. Place the top halves of the rolls to close the sandwiches.

6 Let the sandwiches set for 1 to 2 minutes in the turned-off oven before slicing in half with a serrated bread knife. Serve the sandwich halves warm on a large platter with ketchup and/or hot sauce.

NEW YORK JETS

Italian Sausage and Peppers Sandwiches

PREP TIME: 20 minutes

COOK TIME: 45 minutes

YIELD: 12 large sandwiches (24 sandwich halves)

---

12 large mild or hot Italian sausages (5 ounces, or 142 g, per sausage)

1 tablespoon vegetable oil

6 large bell peppers (mixed colors), cut into strips

4 large yellow onions, thinly sliced

2 teaspoons dried oregano

2 teaspoons dried basil

Salt and black pepper

12 (6- to 8-inch, or 15- to 20-cm) Italian sub rolls

12 deli slices provolone cheese

¾ cup (75 g) grated Parmesan cheese, for garnishing

Potato chips, for serving (optional)

Italian sausage with onions and peppers is a beloved regional dish in New York and Northern New Jersey, particularly linked to the area's Italian American heritage. This simple yet flavorful meal is a staple at festivals, street fairs, and delis, showcasing the vibrant Italian food culture that has shaped the region. The sausages are usually grilled or seared until juicy, paired with sautéed bell peppers and onions, and served in a crusty roll, creating a hearty sandwich that embodies comfort and tradition.

1 Preheat the oven to 375°F (190°C).

2 Slightly pierce each sausage in a few places with a fork to prevent them from rupturing while cooking. Place the sausages on a rimmed baking sheet lined with parchment paper.

3 Bake for 20 to 25 minutes, turning halfway through, until browned and fully cooked to an internal temperature of at least 160°F (70°C). Keep the sausages warm. Alternatively, to get more flavor, sear the sausages in a hot cast-iron skillet on the stovetop (or cook on a grill) over medium-high heat for 8 to 10 minutes, until browned on all sides and fully cooked to an internal temperature of at least 160°F (70°C). Remove the sausages from the heat and keep warm on a platter covered with aluminum foil.

4 While the sausages cook, heat the vegetable oil in a large skillet or Dutch oven over medium heat. Add the bell peppers and onions and cook, stirring often, for 10 to 12 minutes, until softened and lightly caramelized; they should appear golden brown. Season with the oregano, basil, and salt and pepper to taste, then cook for an additional 2 to 3 minutes.

5 Preheat the oven broiler. Slice the Italian rolls open without cutting all the way through. Place the rolls, insides facing up, on baking sheets. Lay 1 slice of provolone cheese across both sides of each roll and broil for 1 to 2 minutes, until the cheese is melted.

6 Fill one side of the roll with the cooked peppers and onions. Place a whole cooked sausage on the other side of the roll, then put the sandwich together. Cut each sandwich in half for serving. Sprinkle each half with some with grated Parmesan cheese and serve warm with potato chips (if using).

★ AFC ★ WEST

DENVER BRONCOS

JOHNNY SLIDERS WITH JALAPEÑO CREAM CHEESE 75

PORK CHILI VERDE 76

KANSAS CITY CHIEFS

CHEESY CORN WITH SMOKED BACON 79

BURNT ENDS SANDWICHES 80

LAS VEGAS RAIDERS

SHRIMP COCKTAIL PLATTER 83

LATE NIGHT STEAK AND EGGS WITH HASH BROWNS 84

LOS ANGELES CHARGERS

ELOTE (LA STREET CORN) 87

FISH TACOS 88

DENVER
BRONCOS

Johnny Sliders with Jalapeño Cream Cheese

PREP TIME: 20 minutes

COOK TIME: 20 minutes

YIELD: 24 sliders

JALAPEÑO CREAM CHEESE

8 ounces (227 g) cream cheese, softened

¼ cup (60 ml) mayonnaise

2 or 3 fresh jalapeños, finely chopped (seeds removed for less heat)

1 tablespoon fresh lime juice

½ teaspoon garlic powder

Salt and black pepper

SLIDERS

1 large white onion, thinly sliced

1 tablespoon vegetable oil

Salt and black pepper

3 pounds (1.4 kg) ground beef (80/20)

12 deli slices Swiss cheese, cut in half

12 deli slices American cheese, cut in half

24 slider buns

FOR SERVING

French fries (optional)

The Johnny Burger is a celebrated regional favorite in Denver, known for its indulgent combination of flavors and textures. Originating and still served at My Brother's Bar, Denver's oldest and most iconic bar (founded as a saloon in 1873), the Johnny Burger features a juicy beef patty generously topped with a delightful blend of Swiss and American cheeses, along with a jalapeño cream cheese spread. This combination not only adds richness but also a hint of spice that elevates the classic burger experience. Grilled onions are piled high on top, adding a satisfying sweet element that perfectly complements the savory flavors. This recipe presents the burger in slider form as an appetizer, perfect for sharing.

1 To make the jalapeño cream cheese: In a medium bowl, mix the cream cheese and mayonnaise until smooth. Add the jalapeños, lime juice, garlic powder, and a pinch each of salt and black pepper. Mix until well combined. Adjust seasoning to taste.

2 To make the sliders: Heat a large skillet over medium-high heat. Toss the onions in a bowl with the vegetable oil and salt and pepper to taste until well coated. Add the onions to the skillet and cook for 10 to 12 minutes, stirring often, until they are soft and caramelized. Remove from the heat.

3 Heat a griddle or the same skillet the onions were cooked in over medium-high heat. Divide the ground beef into 24 equal portions (about 2.5 ounces, or 71 g, each) and shape into patties. Season both sides with salt and pepper.

4 Cook the patties, in batches, for 3 to 4 minutes per side, until they reach the desired level of doneness. Place a half slice of Swiss cheese and a half slice of American cheese on top of each patty during the last minute of cooking to melt.

5 Slice the slider buns horizontally and toast on the still-hot skillet over medium-high heat until golden brown. Spread a generous layer of jalapeño cream cheese on the bottom halves of the buns. Place the cooked patties on top of the cream cheese, followed by a spoonful of the grilled onions. Add the top halves of the bun to each slider.

6 Arrange the Johnny Burger sliders on a large platter. Serve with french fries (if using).

DENVER BRONCOS

Pork Chili Verde

PREP TIME: 20 minutes

COOK TIME: 2 hours

YIELD: 12 servings

Pork chili verde, often simply referred to as "green chili or chile," has deep roots in Colorado's culinary landscape, particularly in Denver. It showcases the state's affinity for green chili peppers, especially Mosco peppers from Pueblo, Colorado, which are renowned for their rich flavor and meaty texture and rival Hatch peppers from New Mexico. Traditionally made with tender chunks of pork simmered in a flavorful green sauce, the dish reflects the region's love for bold, hearty flavors.

CHILI

2 tablespoons vegetable oil

3 pounds (1.4 kg) pork shoulder or pork butt, cut into 1-inch (2.5 cm) cubes

1 large onion, diced

4 cloves garlic, minced

2 jalapeños, diced small (seeds removed for less heat)

4 cups (600 g) roasted, peeled, and chopped Mosco or Hatch green chili peppers (if you cannot find Mosco or Hatch chilies, use Anaheim peppers)

1 cup (55g) fresh or canned chopped tomatillos

2 cups (480 ml) chicken broth

2 teaspoons ground cumin

2 teaspoons dried oregano

1 teaspoon smoked paprika

1 teaspoon salt, or to taste

½ teaspoon black pepper

RICE

2 cups (370 g) long-grain white rice

4 cups (960 ml) low-sodium chicken broth

Salt

1 tablespoon butter (optional)

FOR GARNISHING AND SERVING

½ cup (20 g) chopped fresh cilantro

Lime wedges

1 **To make the chili:** In a large pot or Dutch oven, heat the vegetable oil over medium-high heat. Add the pork in batches, browning on all sides for 5 to 7 minutes. Remove the pork from the pot.

2 To the same pot, add the onions and cook, stirring often, for about 5 minutes, or until translucent. Add the garlic and jalapeños, cooking for an additional 2 to 3 minutes, until fragrant.

3 Add the browned pork back into the pot. Add the Hatch chilies, tomatillos, chicken broth, cumin, oregano, smoked paprika, salt, and pepper. Stir to combine, ensuring the pork is well coated with the spices and vegetables. Bring the mixture to a boil, then reduce the heat to low. Cover the pot and let simmer for 1 hour and 30 minutes to 2 hours, until the pork is tender and easily shreds with a fork.

4 **While the chili is simmering, make the rice:** Rinse the rice under cold water until the water runs clear. In a separate large pot, combine the rice and chicken broth and season with salt to taste. Bring to a boil, then reduce the heat to low, cover, and let simmer for 18 to 20 minutes, until the rice is tender and the liquid is absorbed. Fluff the rice with a fork and stir in the butter (if using).

5 Taste the chili and adjust the seasoning with salt and/or pepper if necessary. Ladle the chili into bowls alongside a scoop of rice. Garnish with the chopped cilantro and serve with lime wedges for squeezing.

KANSAS
CITY
CHIEFS

Cheesy Corn with Smoked Bacon

PREP TIME: 20 minutes

COOK TIME: 35 minutes

YIELD: 20 servings

8 ears fresh sweet corn (about 5 cups, or 725 g, corn kernels), shucked

8 slices smoked bacon

1 cup (240 g) cream cheese, softened

1 cup (240 ml) sour cream

1 cup (115 g) shredded sharp cheddar cheese

1 cup (115 g) shredded Monterey Jack cheese

½ cup (120 ml) whole milk

½ teaspoon garlic powder

½ teaspoon onion powder

½ teaspoon smoked paprika

¼ teaspoon cayenne pepper

Salt and black pepper

Nonstick cooking spray

¼ cup (11 g) chopped fresh chives or sliced scallions, for garnishing

Tortilla chips, for serving

Kansas City cheesy corn reflects the heartiness and creativity of Midwestern cuisine. This indulgent side dish typically features sweet corn mixed with a rich, creamy cheese sauce often enriched with spices and seasonings. Corn is a staple crop of the state, making it a natural choice for local cooks to elevate with dairy and flavor. The dish has grown popular at barbecues, family gatherings, and potlucks, embodying the communal spirit of Kansas City dining. You can find cheesy corn served at iconic establishments like Jack Stack, which is known for inventing the dish.

1   Preheat the oven to 350°F (175°C). Using a sharp knife, cut the kernels off the cobs by standing each ear of corn upright in a large bowl and running the knife down the sides to remove the kernels. To "milk the cob," after cutting off the kernels, hold the cob upright in the bowl and use the back of the knife to scrape down the sides of the cob; this will release the milky juice, adding more flavor and creaminess to the dish.

2   In a large skillet over medium heat, cook the bacon until crispy. Remove the bacon from the skillet and place it on a paper towel–lined plate. Let cool, then chop into small pieces.

3   In a large bowl, combine the corn kernels and their milk, the cream cheese, sour cream, cheddar cheese, Monterey Jack cheese, and milk. Stir in the garlic powder, onion powder, smoked paprika, cayenne pepper, and salt and black pepper to taste. Mix until well combined. Gently fold in the chopped bacon.

4   Grease a 9 x 13-inch (23 x 33 cm) baking dish with nonstick spray. Transfer the corn mixture to the prepared dish, evenly spreading it. Bake for 25 to 30 minutes, until the top is golden and bubbly. Remove from the oven and let cool slightly.

5   Garnish with the chopped chives or scallions and serve with tortilla chips for dipping.

EXTRA POINT

This recipe is always an excellent side dish served alongside Kansas City barbecue.

KANSAS CITY CHIEFS

Burnt Ends Sandwiches

PREP TIME: 20 minutes

COOK TIME: 6 to 8 hours (includes smoking or oven cooking and resting time)

YIELD: 12 sandwiches

BURNT ENDS

5 pounds (2.3 kg) lean beef brisket (point cut)

2 tablespoons kosher salt

2 tablespoons black pepper

1 tablespoon smoked paprika

1 tablespoon garlic powder

1 tablespoon onion powder

1 cup (240 ml) Kansas City–style barbecue sauce

½ cup (120 ml) apple cider vinegar

¼ cup (55 g) brown sugar

1 tablespoon Worcestershire sauce

SANDWICHES

12 soft sandwich buns or brioche rolls

Dill pickle slices, for garnishing

Kansas City–style barbecue sauce, for drizzling

FOR SERVING

Kansas City–style barbecue sauce

The burnt ends sandwich is a Kansas City staple, originating from the practice of utilizing the flavorful trimmings from brisket. These small, well-cooked pieces were once considered scraps, but their rich, smoky flavor and tender texture quickly gained popularity among barbecue enthusiasts. Burnt ends are typically made by slow-smoking a beef brisket until it's fork-tender, then cubing the well-cooked ends, coating them in barbecue sauce, and returning them to the smoker for further caramelization. This recipe presents the dish as a portable, delectable barbecue sandwich, breaking down the full brisket point into chunks to make the burnt ends.

1 To make the burnt ends: Trim excess fat from the brisket, leaving about ¼ inch (6 mm) for flavor. In a small bowl, mix the salt, pepper, smoked paprika, garlic powder, and onion powder until well combined. Rub the dry-rub mixture all over the brisket, ensuring even coverage.

2 If smoking, preheat the smoker to 225°F (107°C). Place the seasoned brisket in the smoker and cook until the internal temperature reaches 195°F (90°C), 6 to 8 hours. Once the brisket is cooked, remove it from the smoker and let rest for 30 minutes to 1 hour. If oven cooking, preheat the oven to 300°F (150°C). Place the seasoned brisket in a roasting pan and cover it tightly with aluminum foil. Roast in the oven for 4 to 5 hours, until the internal temperature reaches 195°F (90°C). Remove the brisket from the oven and let rest for 30 minutes to 1 hour. Keep the oven on.

3 Cut the brisket into 1-inch (2.5 cm) cubes. In a large bowl, mix the 1 cup (240 ml) barbecue sauce, vinegar, brown sugar, and Worcestershire sauce until well combined. Add the cubed brisket and toss until evenly coated.

4 To finish in the smoker, place the coated cubes back into the smoker to cook for an additional 1 to 2 hours, stirring occasionally, until the burnt ends are caramelized and tender. To finish in the oven, spread the coated cubes on a rimmed baking sheet lined with parchment paper and bake at 300°F (150°C) for about 1 hour, or until caramelized.

5 To assemble the sandwiches: Slice the sandwich buns horizontally and toast lightly on the grill or in the oven, if desired. Pile the warm burnt ends onto the bottom halves of the buns. Drizzle additional barbecue sauce over the top, then add pickles. Top with the other halves of the buns and serve immediately with more barbecue sauce.

LAS VEGAS RAIDERS

Shrimp Cocktail Platter

PREP TIME: 20 minutes

COOK TIME: 5 minutes

YIELD: 15 servings

SHRIMP

3 quarts (12 cups, or 2.8L) water

1 lemon, cut in half

2 bay leaves

2 tablespoons kosher salt

1 tablespoon black peppercorns

Ice, for chilling shrimp

45 jumbo (16/20) shrimp, peeled and deveined

Lemon wedges

COCKTAIL SAUCE

1 cup (240 ml) ketchup

2 tablespoons prepared horseradish, or to taste

1 tablespoon fresh lemon juice

1 teaspoon Worcestershire sauce

1 teaspoon favorite hot sauce (I like Tabasco)

¼ teaspoon kosher salt

¼ teaspoon black pepper

FOR SERVING

Lemon wedges

The Las Vegas shrimp cocktail holds a special place in the city's food scene, symbolizing the affordable luxury that once defined the Strip. First introduced at the Golden Gate Casino in 1959, shrimp cocktail quickly became a staple, offering a lavish experience for just fifty cents. For decades, this dish remained a culinary icon, with its price barely increasing until 1999, when it rose to ninety-nine cents. The shrimp cocktail is more than just an appetizer—it's a reflection of the city's rich culinary heritage.

1 Place a large serving platter in the refrigerator to chill for serving.

2 To make the shrimp: Fill a large pot with the water, lemon halves, bay leaves, salt, and peppercorns and bring to a rolling simmer. Fill a bowl with ice (not ice water!).

3 Add the shrimp and cook for 2 to 4 minutes, until pink and opaque and the internal temperature is 145°F (63°C). (Avoid overcooking to maintain tenderness.) Remove the shrimp from the boiling water and immediately transfer them to the prepared bowl of ice. Toss the shrimp in the ice to quickly cool them down and preserve their flavor. Leave them on ice for about 3 minutes, then drain and pat dry with paper towels. Keep cold.

4 To make the cocktail sauce: In a medium bowl, mix the ketchup, horseradish, lemon juice, Worcestershire sauce, hot sauce, salt, and pepper until well combined. Adjust the seasoning to taste.

5 Transfer the cocktail sauce to a serving bowl. On the large, chilled serving platter, place the bowl in the center. Arrange the shrimp around the cocktail sauce bowl, along with the lemon wedges for squeezing.

LAS VEGAS RAIDERS

Late Night Steak and Eggs with Hash Browns

PREP TIME: 20 minutes

COOK TIME: 30 minutes

YIELD: 12 servings

HASH BROWNS

6 large russet potatoes, peeled and grated (about 3 pounds, or 1.4 kg)

2 tablespoons vegetable oil

1 medium onion, finely chopped

Salt and black pepper

3 tablespoons olive oil

STEAK AND EGGS

12 strip steaks (6 to 8 ounces, or 170 to 227 g, each)

2 teaspoons garlic powder

Kosher salt and black pepper

3 tablespoons vegetable oil

6 tablespoons unsalted butter, divided

24 large eggs

Steak and eggs goes back to the early days of the space program. Traditionally, astronauts consumed steak and eggs as their pre-launch meal, starting with the Mercury missions in the early 1960s. The high-protein dish was chosen to provide sustained energy for the demanding journey ahead. It carried over to wider American culture, where the hearty meal became associated with endurance, hard work, and adventure—qualities embodied by Las Vegas. In Vegas, steak and eggs became a late-night favorite during the 1950s and '60s, as casinos sought to keep gamblers fueled and at the tables into the early morning hours.

1 To make the hash browns: Rinse the grated potatoes in cold water to remove excess starch. Drain well and pat dry with paper towels.

2 In a large skillet, heat the 2 tablespoons vegetable oil over medium heat. Add the onion and cook, stirring often, until softened, 3 to 4 minutes. Add the grated potatoes to the skillet and press down to form an even layer. Season with salt and pepper to taste and cook without stirring for 5 to 7 minutes, until the bottom is golden brown and crispy. Flip the hash browns over in sections or use a spatula to flip the entire hash brown cake. Add the olive oil around the edges. Continue cooking for another 5 to 7 minutes, until golden and crispy on both sides. Remove from the pan and keep warm and crispy under aluminum foil.

3 To make the steak and eggs: Pat the steaks dry with paper towels. Season both sides with the garlic powder and kosher salt and pepper to taste.

4 In two large skillets or cast-iron pans, heat 1½ tablespoons each of the vegetable oil and butter in each pan over medium-high heat. Add the steaks, in batches, being careful not to overcrowd the pans. Sear each steak for 2 to 3 minutes per side for medium-rare, or cook to desired doneness. Remove the steaks from the pans, place them on a plate, cover with foil, and let rest for 5 to 7 minutes.

5 In a separate nonstick skillet, melt the remaining 3 tablespoons butter over medium heat. Cook the eggs, in batches, sunny-side up (or to your preference). Season with kosher salt and pepper to taste.

6 Serve each steak with 2 eggs on the side and a portion of hash browns.

LOS ANGELES CHARGERS

Elote (LA Street Corn)

PREP TIME: 10 minutes

COOK TIME: 15 minutes

YIELD: 15 ears of corn

15 ears fresh sweet corn, shucked

1 cup (240 ml) mayonnaise

1 cup (240 ml) sour cream

3 tablespoons fresh lime juice (about 3 limes)

3 tablespoons chili powder, or to taste

1 teaspoon garlic powder

½ teaspoon kosher salt

½ teaspoon black pepper

1 cup (150 g) crumbled cotija cheese, (or substitute with grated Parmesan cheese), plus more for finishing

Chopped fresh cilantro, for garnishing

Lime wedges, for serving

Los Angeles street corn, or elote, is a beloved Mexican American street food that has become a staple in the city's vibrant food culture. Elote traditionally features grilled corn on the cob slathered in a creamy mixture of mayonnaise, lime juice, chili powder, and cotija cheese. This dish reflects the culinary fusion found in Los Angeles, where Mexican flavors and local ingredients come together, making it a popular choice among street vendors and at summer barbecues. The popular Corn Man stand in Lincoln Heights offers a delicious take on the classic recipe, ensuring that the dish continues to evolve. Additionally, local festivals and street fairs frequently showcase elote, allowing attendees to enjoy this delicious treat in a lively atmosphere.

1 Preheat the grill to medium-high heat. Grill the corn on the cob for 10 to 15 minutes, turning occasionally, until the kernels are tender and charred in spots. Remove from the grill and let cool slightly. Alternatively, you can roast the corn in an oven preheated to 400°F (205°C) for 25 to 30 minutes, turning occasionally, until slightly charred.

2 While the corn is roasting, mix the mayonnaise, sour cream, and lime juice in a small bowl until well combined.

3 In another small bowl, mix the chili powder, garlic powder, salt, and pepper until well combined.

4 Spread a thin layer of the mayonnaise–sour cream mixture on every side of the grilled corn ears. Sprinkle the corn ears generously with cotija cheese, followed by the chili powder mixture.

5 To finish, sprinkle additional cotija cheese over the coated corn and garnish with chopped cilantro.

6 Arrange the elote on a serving platter and serve with lime wedges for squeezing.

LOS ANGELES CHARGERS

Fish Tacos

PREP TIME: 20 minutes

COOK TIME: 15 minutes

YIELD: 15 tacos

SLAW

4 cups (380 g) thinly sliced cabbage

1 cup (110 g) shredded carrots

½ cup (55 g) thinly sliced red onion

¼ cup (10 g) chopped fresh cilantro

¼ cup (60 ml) fresh lime juice

1 tablespoon olive oil

Salt and black pepper

FISH

1 cup (125 g) all-purpose flour

1 cup (180 g) cornmeal

2 teaspoons chili powder

1 teaspoon paprika

1 teaspoon ground cumin

1 teaspoon garlic powder

1 teaspoon salt

½ teaspoon black pepper

1 cup (240 ml) buttermilk

3 pounds (1.4 kg) white fish fillets (such as tilapia or halibut)

Vegetable oil, for frying

TACOS

15 (6-inch, or 15-cm) corn tortillas

1½ cups (270 g) pico de gallo or salsa

3 avocados, sliced (optional)

Lime wedges, for serving

Fish tacos have become a beloved staple of Los Angeles' vibrant food truck scene, reflecting the city's diverse culinary influences. Originating from Baja California, Mexico, fish tacos traditionally featured battered and fried fish wrapped in corn tortillas and topped with fresh ingredients like cabbage, salsa, and creamy sauces. As the dish made its way across the border, it adapted to incorporate local flavors and styles, becoming a favorite among Angelenos seeking fresh and flavorful street food. Notable LA spots for fish tacos include Baja California Tacos on Hillhurst Avenue, known for its crispy fried fish and homemade sauces, and Mariscos Jalisco, famous for its succulent shrimp tacos. These food trucks not only serve delicious fish tacos but also embody the city's spirit of innovation and community, making them essential stops for both locals and visitors alike.

1 **To make the slaw:** In a large bowl, combine the cabbage, carrots, red onion, and cilantro. In a separate small bowl, whisk together the lime juice, olive oil, salt, and pepper. Pour the dressing over the slaw mixture and toss to combine. Set aside to allow the flavors to meld. (Make the slaw no more than 30 minutes before serving the tacos.)

2 **To make the fish:** Set up a breading station by mixing the flour, cornmeal, chili powder, paprika, cumin, garlic powder, salt, and pepper in a shallow dish until well combined and pouring the buttermilk into another shallow dish. Dip each fish fillet first into the buttermilk, allowing excess to drip off, then coat with the flour mixture, pressing to adhere.

3 In a large skillet or frying pan, heat about 1 inch (2.5 cm) of vegetable oil over medium-high heat. Once the oil is hot, carefully add the coated fish fillets, in batches, frying for 3 to 4 minutes per side, until golden brown and cooked through. Transfer to a paper towel–lined plate.

4 **To assemble the tacos:** In a separate, dry skillet, warm the corn tortillas, one or two at a time, over medium heat for about 30 seconds per side, or until soft and bendable. On each warmed tortilla, place a piece of fried fish, a generous scoop of slaw, and a spoonful of pico de gallo. Add slices of avocado (if using).

5 Serve the fish tacos with lime wedges for squeezing.

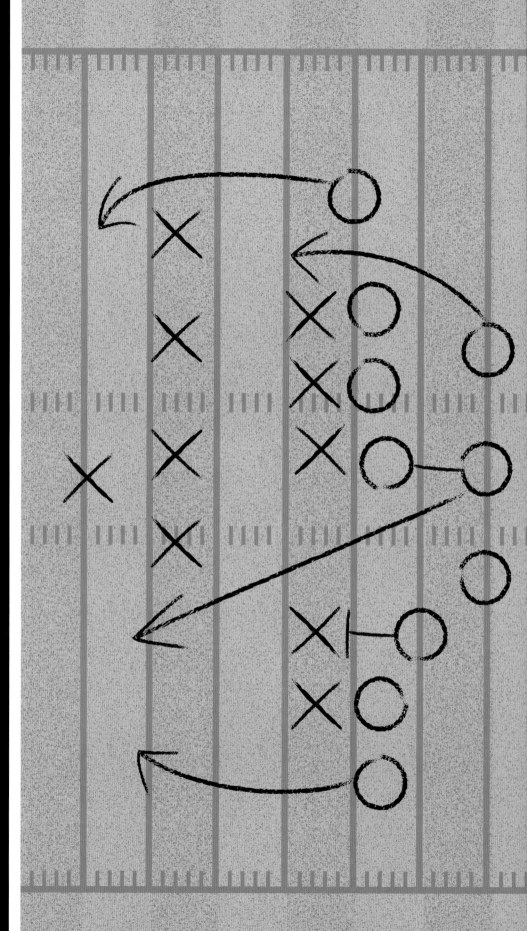

NFC

NFC NORTH

CHICAGO BEARS
DETROIT LIONS
GREEN BAY PACKERS
MINNESOTA VIKINGS

NFC SOUTH

ATLANTA FALCONS
CAROLINA PANTHERS
NEW ORLEANS SAINTS
TAMPA BAY BUCCANEERS

NFC EAST

DALLAS COWBOYS
NEW YORK GIANTS
PHILADELPHIA EAGLES
WASHINGTON COMMANDERS

NFC WEST

ARIZONA CARDINALS
LOS ANGELES RAMS
SAN FRANCISCO 49ERS
SEATTLE SEAHAWKS

★ NFC NORTH ★

CHICAGO BEARS

MINI DEEP-DISH PIZZAS 95

CHICKEN VESUVIO 96

DETROIT LIONS

CORNED BEEF EGG ROLLS 99

CONEY DOGS 100

GREEN BAY PACKERS

FRIED CHEESE CURDS 103

BEER-BRAISED BRATWURSTS 104

MINNESOTA VIKINGS

JUICY LUCY SLIDERS 107

TATER TOT HOTDISH 108

Mini Deep-Dish Pizzas

PREP TIME: 40 minutes

COOK TIME: 18 minutes

YIELD: 12 mini pizzas

Deep-dish pizza is a quintessential Chicago delicacy, characterized by its thick, hearty layers. This iconic dish was first created in the 1940s by Ike Sewell and Ric Riccardo, who sought to offer a more substantial alternative to the standard thin-crust pizza. They opened Pizzeria Uno in downtown Chicago, where they debuted their deep-dish pizza. The following recipe presents a smaller version of the classic dish to be eaten as an appetizer.

PIZZA SAUCE

1 teaspoon olive oil

½ small yellow onion, minced

2 cloves garlic, minced

2 (28-ounce, or 794-g) cans Italian-style crushed tomatoes

½ teaspoon sugar

1 teaspoon dried oregano

½ teaspoon red pepper flakes

1½ teaspoons kosher salt

¼ cup (10 g) roughly chopped fresh basil leaves

PIZZAS

Nonstick cooking spray

2 (13.8-ounce, or 391-g) tubes prepared pizza dough (such as Pillsbury)

12 thin slices mozzarella cheese

36 slices pepperoni

½ cup (50 g) grated Parmesan cheese, plus more for garnishing

1 Preheat the oven to 375°F (190°C). Spray a 12-cup muffin pan with nonstick spray and set aside.

2 To make the pizza sauce: Heat a deep saucepan over medium-high heat and add the olive oil. Add the onion and cook, stirring often, until it just turns translucent. Add the garlic and cook until fragrant. Do not brown the onion and garlic.

3 Add both cans of tomatoes, the sugar, oregano, and red pepper flakes. Over medium heat, bring the sauce to a simmer. Reduce the heat to low and let simmer, uncovered, for 40 minutes, stirring occasionally, until the sauce thickens. Remove the sauce from the heat and stir in the salt and fresh basil.

4 To make the pizzas: Roll out the pizza dough flat and press until it is slightly thinner. Using the rim of a juice glass, cut out 12 circles of dough. Use the same glass to cut out 24 circles of mozzarella from the slices, 2 circles per slice. Press each dough circle into a muffin cup, making sure to press it all the way up the sides.

5 Place 1 circle of mozzarella on each dough. Top with 3 slices of pepperoni. Top with another slice of mozzarella. Fill the rest of the cup with pizza sauce almost up to the top. Sprinkle each cup with grated Parmesan cheese.

6 Bake for 16 to 18 minutes, until the crust is crispy and the cheese is melted and golden brown. Remove the muffin pan from the oven and let the pizzas sit for 2 minutes. Carefully slide each mini deep-dish pizza from the pan onto a large platter. Garnish with more grated Parmesan. Serve immediately.

CHICAGO BEARS

Italian Beef Sandwiches

PREP TIME: 20 minutes

COOK TIME: 4 hours, plus overnight chill

YIELD: 12 servings

The Italian beef sandwich is a Chicago staple, born from the city's working-class roots in the early twentieth century. Originally created by Italian immigrants looking to stretch tough cuts of beef, the meat is slow-cooked in a seasoned au jus, cooled, sliced thin, and then reheated in its flavorful juices. Traditionally served on a sturdy Italian roll, the sandwich can be ordered "dry," "wet," or "dipped," meaning the bread can range from lightly moistened to fully soaked in the rich broth. Many people like to top their sandwiches with sweet bell peppers and/or spicy giardiniera for an extra punch of flavor. For this recipe, the beef needs to be prepared a day in advance of your game-day event.

BEEF

5 pounds (2.3 kg) boneless beef chuck roast or rump roast

1 teaspoon salt

1 teaspoon black pepper

2 tablespoons vegetable oil

4 cups (960 ml) beef broth

1 tablespoon dried Italian seasoning

2 teaspoons garlic powder

1 teaspoon onion powder

½ teaspoon red pepper flakes

8 whole pepperoncini

1 bay leaf

SAUTÉED BELL PEPPERS (OPTIONAL)

3 large green bell peppers, cut into strips

1 tablespoon olive oil

Salt and black pepper

SANDWICHES

12 Italian or French rolls

12 slices provolone cheese (optional)

1 cup (130 g) hot giardiniera (Italian pickled vegetable relish; I use Mezzetta brand) (optional))

1 To make the beef (a day in advance): Preheat the oven to 300°F (150°C). Season the beef roast with the 1 tablespoon each salt and black pepper.

2 In a large oven-safe pot or Dutch oven, heat the vegetable oil over medium-high heat. Add the roast and sear on all sides until browned, 3 to 4 minutes per side. Add the beef broth, 1 cup (240 ml) of water, Italian seasoning, garlic powder, onion powder, red pepper flakes, pepperoncini, and bay leaf to the pot. Cover and transfer to the oven.

3 Roast until the beef's internal temperature reaches 195°F (90°C), about 3 hours and 30 minutes to 4 hours. Remove the beef from the pot and let cool to room temperature. Strain the cooking juices into a container with a lid, keeping the pepperoncini in the juices and discarding the bay leaf. Cover and refrigerate overnight. Wrap the cooled beef tightly in plastic wrap or aluminum foil and refrigerate overnight.

4 The next day, remove the chilled beef from the refrigerator and slice it very thinly against the grain using a sharp knife or meat slicer (you can also shred it with two forks, if you prefer).

5 In a large pot over medium high heat, reheat the reserved juices (au jus) with pepperoncini over low heat until hot. Add the sliced beef and let it soak in the juices for a few minutes to warm through.

6 Meanwhile, make the sautéed bell peppers (if using): In a large skillet, heat the olive oil over medium heat. Add the bell peppers, season with salt and pepper to taste, and sauté until tender, about 5 to 7 minutes. Remove from the heat

7 To assemble the sandwiches: Slice the rolls lengthwise, keeping one side intact. If using, place a slice of provolone cheese inside each roll, then use tongs to pile warm, juice-soaked beef into each roll. If using, top with sautéed bell peppers and/or a spoonful of giardiniera.

8 Serve the sandwiches hot on a large platter or wooden cutting board with extra au jus on the side for dipping.

DETROIT LIONS

Corned Beef Egg Rolls

PREP TIME: 15 minutes

COOK TIME: 30 minutes

YIELD: 12 egg rolls

About 5 cups (1.2 L) vegetable oil, for frying

1 pound (454 g) deli-sliced corned beef

1 pound (454 g) deli-sliced Swiss cheese

2 egg whites

12 wonton wrappers

Duck sauce, for dipping

½ cup (30 g) thinly sliced scallions, for garnishing

Corned beef egg rolls are a distinctive and popular dish in Detroit, Michigan, representing a fusion of cultures and flavors that reflect the city's diverse culinary landscape. They were created in the late 1970s by Kim White, a Vietnamese immigrant, whose first job was working in a corned beef deli. In Detroit, corned beef egg rolls can be found at several popular spots. Corned Beef, the establishment White founded that first introduced the dish, remains the go-to place for these egg rolls. They offer several versions, including ones with cheese and cabbage and even a variation with spicy jalapeños, all served fresh and hot.

1 In a large cast-iron skillet, heat the oil over medium heat until it reaches 350°F (175°C). Set a cooling rack over a rimmed baking sheet next to the stove.

2 While the oil is heating, stack the corned beef slices and shred thin with a chef's knife. Stack all the cheese slices in a pile and slice into thin shreds. Whisk the egg whites in a small bowl.

3 Lay a wonton wrapper on a clean surface with a corner facing you, like a diamond. Place 1 tablespoon of cheese in the middle, then place 2 tablespoons of shredded corned beef on top of the cheese.

4 Fold the bottom corner up over the filling, fold the sides inward, and roll tightly. Brush the top corner with some whisked egg white to seal the egg roll. Repeat with the remaining wrappers and filling.

5 Carefully fry 3 or 4 egg rolls at a time, for 3 to 4 minutes, flipping them halfway through, until golden brown and crispy. Transfer to the prepared cooling rack.

6 Place the duck sauce in a small bowl in the center of a large platter. Arrange the hot egg rolls around the duck sauce and garnish with the sliced scallions.

DETROIT LIONS

Coney Dogs

PREP TIME: 10 minutes

COOK TIME: 45 minutes

YIELD: 8 Coney Dogs

CHILI (CONEY SAUCE)

1 pound (454 g) 90% lean ground beef

1 (15-ounce, or 425-gram) can tomato puree

½ cup (120 ml) water

2 tablespoons Worcestershire sauce

1 cup (125 g) finely chopped white onion

2 cloves garlic, minced

1½ tablespoons chili powder

1½ teaspoons kosher salt

½ teaspoon onion powder

½ teaspoon granulated garlic

½ teaspoon black pepper

¼ teaspoon white sugar

2 dashes Tabasco sauce

3 tablespoons yellow mustard

HOT DOGS

8 beef hot dogs (I like Sabrett)

8 hot dog buns

Finely chopped white onion, for garnishing

Yellow mustard, for garnishing

FOR SERVING

French fries

Coney dogs are a quintessential part of Detroit's culinary identity. The dish has its roots in the early twentieth century, when Greek immigrants began serving hot dogs topped with a special beef chili, yellow mustard, and chopped onions. Despite the name, Coney dogs have no direct connection to Coney Island in Brooklyn, New York; rather, the name was likely adopted to evoke the all-American hot dog tradition. The defining feature of a Detroit Coney dog is the chili. The key is to use a very lean ground beef, to avoid a greasy chili. In Detroit, two rival establishments, located next to each other downtown, are iconic for serving legendary Coney dogs: Lafayette Coney Island and American Coney Island.

1 To make the chili: Heat a large pot over medium-high heat. Break the ground beef into crumbles and then add it to the pot. Sear the beef, break it up with a wooden spoon, until fully cooked.

2 Stir in the tomato puree, water, Worcestershire sauce, onion, minced garlic, chili powder, salt, onion powder, granulated garlic, pepper, sugar, Tabasco sauce, and mustard. Make sure to mix thoroughly.

3 Reduce the heat to low, cover, and let simmer for 30 minutes. Uncover and let simmer, stirring occasionally, for an additional 10 minutes to thicken the chili.

4 To make the hot dogs: For Detroit-style hot dogs, steam them in a steamer pot for steaming vegetables. Fill the pot with water and place the hot dogs in the steamer basket. Bring the water to a boil and steam until the hot dogs reach an internal temperature of 170°F (77°C). (You can also boil them to achieve this consistency.) Warm the buns slightly in the microwave for 15 seconds, then place the hot dogs in the buns. Top each hot dog with chili (Concy sauce), diced white onion, and mustard. Serve immediately on a large platter with french fries.

Fried Cheese Curds

PREP TIME: 10 minutes

COOK TIME: 1 to 2 minutes

YIELD: 8 servings

Fried cheese curds are a beloved regional delicacy in Green Bay, reflecting the state's deep-rooted cheese-making heritage. The fresh, young curds, which are separated from the whey during the cheese-making process, are known for their mild flavor and distinctive squeak when eaten fresh. In Wisconsin, these curds are often battered or breaded and deep-fried to create a crispy, golden exterior that contrasts with the warm, gooey cheese inside.

8 cups (1.9 L) vegetable oil, for frying

¼ cup (60 ml) whole milk

¾ cup (180 ml) lager beer

1 large egg

½ teaspoon salt

½ teaspoon granulated garlic

½ teaspoon dried oregano

1 cup (125 g) all-purpose flour

1 teaspoon baking powder

2 pounds (907 g) cheese curds, broken apart

Favorite ranch dressing, for serving

1 Heat the oil to 375°F (190°C) in a deep fryer, Dutch oven, or deep cast-iron skillet.

2 In a deep bowl, whisk together the milk, beer, and egg, making sure to completely mix in the egg. In a separate bowl, mix the salt, garlic, oregano, flour, and baking powder until thoroughly combined.

3 Gradually whisk the dry ingredients into the wet ingredients until a smooth, thin batter forms.

4 Place 6 to 8 cheese curds at a time into the batter, stir to coat, and remove with a wire strainer. Shake the curds once or twice to remove excess batter. Carefully fry the curds until golden brown, 1 to 2 minutes. Transfer to a paper towel–lined plate. Repeat with the remaining cheese curds and batter.

5 Serve hot on a large platter with ranch dressing.

GREEN BAY PACKERS

Beer-Braised Bratwursts

PREP TIME: 10 minutes

COOK TIME: 45 to 50 minutes

YIELD: 10 bratwurst

½ cup (115 g, or 1 stick) unsalted butter

3 large yellow onions, julienned

8 cloves garlic, crushed

10 pork bratwurst

15 black peppercorns

2 bay leaves

1 teaspoon caraway seeds

3 (12-ounce, or 355-ml) bottles American-style pilsner beer (I like Miller, but if you really want traditional, use Leinenkugel's)

Cooking oil, for greasing

10 small sub rolls

1 (32-ounce, or 946-ml) jar sauerkraut, chilled

Spicy brown mustard, for serving

Beer-braised bratwurst is a cherished regional favorite in Green Bay, combining two of the state's most iconic products: bratwurst and beer. This dish has its roots in Wisconsin's strong German heritage in which bratwurst sausages were traditionally simmered in beer before being grilled. A popular spot is Kroll's West, a Green Bay institution known for its traditional Wisconsin fare. Kroll's serves brats with all the classic toppings, making it a go-to destination for anyone looking to experience authentic Green Bay flavors.

1 In a deep cast-iron skillet (or Dutch oven), melt the butter over medium-high heat.

2 Add the onions and cook, stirring often, until light golden brown. Add the garlic and cook, stirring often, until the garlic is fragrant and the onions are darker in color.

3 Place the bratwurst on top of the onions and garlic. Add the peppercorns, bay leaves, and caraway seeds. Pour the beer into the skillet; the brats should be fully covered. Bring to a boil, then reduce the heat and let simmer for 30 minutes.

4 While the brats are cooking, get a gas or charcoal grill very hot. Make sure to oil the grill very well. Take the brats out of the skillet and place them right on the grill. Grill the brats on every side until the skin is dark golden brown and slightly crispy, then place the brats back on top of cooked onion-beer mixture.

5 Serving right from the onion-beer mixture, place the cooked onions on one side of the rolls, the sauerkraut on the other side, and the grilled brats in the middle. Top with spicy brown mustard and serve hot.

Juicy Lucy Sliders

PREP TIME: 15 minutes

COOK TIME: 20 minutes

YIELD: 20 sliders

5 pounds (2.3 kg) ground beef (80/20)

20 slices American cheese

Butter, as needed

2 large yellow onions, finely chopped

20 slider buns

Sandwich pickle slices (optional)

French fries and/or onion rings, for serving

The Juicy Lucy is a Minneapolis icon, renowned for its inventive twist on the traditional cheeseburger. Rather than having the cheese on top, this burger features a molten core of cheese stuffed inside the beef patty, which oozes out with each bite. Its origins trace back to the 1950s, though two local spots—Matt's Bar and the 5-8 Club—claim to be the birthplace of this creation. At Matt's Bar, the "Jucy" Lucy is served with American cheese, pickles, and a soft bun, keeping the recipe simple yet satisfying. In contrast, the 5-8 Club allows patrons to choose from different cheeses, like cheddar or Swiss, creating variety in the experience. Both venues serve their burgers with fries or onion rings, making the Juicy Lucy a delicious reflection of Minneapolis's culinary creativity.

1 Divide the beef into forty 2-ounce (57 g) portions; flatten each portion into a patty. Fold a cheese slice into quarters and place it on top of a patty. Top with another patty. Pinch the edges of the patties together, sealing them, making sure there are no holes for the cheese to leak out. Repeat with the remaining patties and cheese.

2 In a large skillet, melt the butter over medium-high heat. Add the onions and cook until dark golden brown.

3 Butter the insides of the slider buns and toast until golden brown.

4 Cooking in batches, place the sliders in a frying pan over medium-high heat. Cook each side for 3 to 6 minutes, until the internal temperature reaches 155°F (68°C). (You will see slightly cheesy-looking juice ooze out.)

5 If you wish, add pickles to the bottom halves of the buns, followed by the fried onions. Top with the cooked burgers and the bun tops. Serve on a large platter with fries and/or onion rings.

MINNESOTA
VIKINGS

Tater Tot Hotdish

PREP TIME: 15 minutes

COOK TIME: 45 minutes

YIELD: 15 servings

Nonstick cooking spray

2 pounds (907 g) ground beef (80/20)

1 large yellow onion, diced small

5 cloves garlic, minced

Salt and black pepper

1½ cups (205 g) frozen corn, thawed

1½ cups (200 g) frozen peas, thawed

1 (10-ounce, or 284-gram) can condensed cheddar cheese soup

2 (10-ounce, or 284-gram) cans condensed cream of mushroom soup

1 cup (240 ml) whole milk

½ teaspoon favorite hot sauce (in Minnesota they use Cry Baby Craig's)

1 pound (454 g) shredded cheddar cheese, divided

1 (2-pound, or 907 g) bag frozen Tater Tots

Side salad and/or crusty bread, for serving

Born out of practicality during the Great Depression, hotdish typically consists of a starch, a protein, vegetables, and a can of condensed soup as a binder. The most iconic version includes Tater Tots as the starch, ground beef as the protein, and vegetables like peas or green beans, all baked together in a creamy sauce until bubbling.

1 Preheat the oven to 350°F (175°C) and lightly grease a 9 x 13-inch (23 x 33 cm) baking dish with nonstick spray.

2 To a large skillet, add the ground beef and season with salt and pepper to taste. Cook over medium heat, breaking up the meat with a wooden spoon, until fully browned. Carefully strain off the grease leaving 1 teaspoon, then add.the onion and garlic and cook over medium heat, stirring often, for 2 to 3 minutes.

3 As the beef browns, combine the corn, peas, both soups, milk, hot sauce, and half the cheese in a large bowl.

4 Add the browned beef to the soup mixture and stir to combine. Spoon the mixture into the prepared baking dish, making sure to spread into an even layer.

5 Top with the remaining cheese, followed by the Tater Tots in a single layer, laying the tots next to each other in rows.

6 Bake for 45 minutes, or until the Tots are golden brown. Serve hot with a side salad and/or crusty bread.

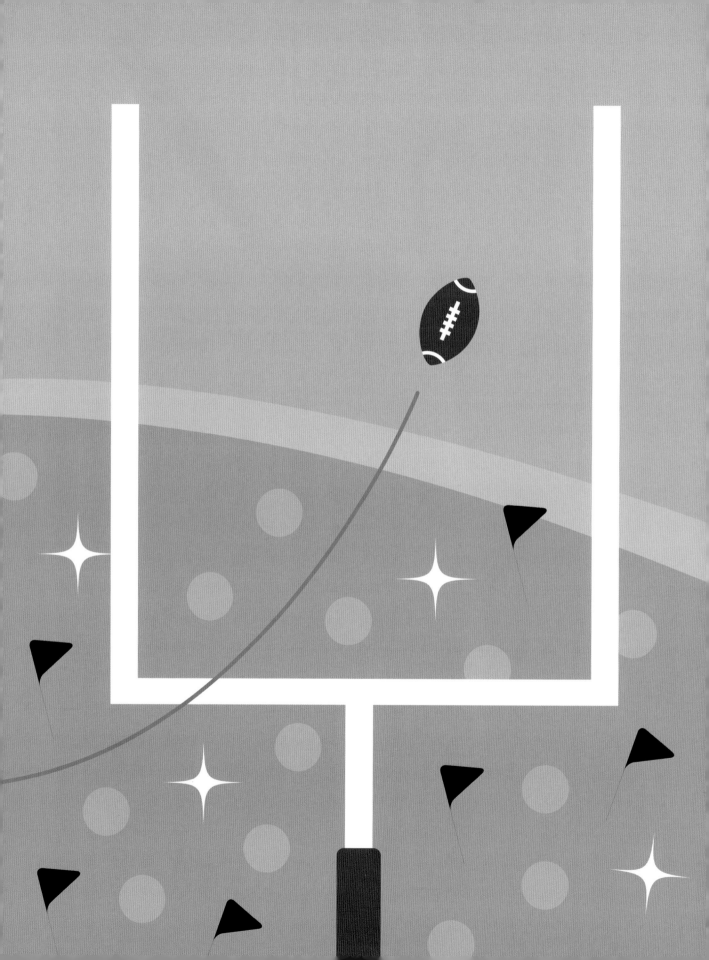

★ NFC ★ SOUTH

ATLANTA FALCONS

MINI CHICKEN-AND-WAFFLE SANDWICHES 113

SHRIMP AND GRITS 114

CAROLINA PANTHERS

BISCUITS WITH FRIED GREEN TOMATOES 117

CAROLINA PULLED PORK
SANDWICHES WITH SLAW 118

NEW ORLEANS SAINTS

MINI FRIED SHRIMP PO'BOYS 121

CHICKEN AND ANDOUILLE SAUSAGE GUMBO 122

TAMPA BAY BUCCANEERS

DEVILED CRAB CROQUETTES 125

BLACKENED FISH SANDWICHESYS 126

ATLANTA FALCONS

Mini Chicken-and-Waffle Sandwiches

PREP TIME: 45 minutes, plus 4 hours marinating

COOK TIME: 1 hour

YIELD: 20 mini sandwiches

Chicken and waffles is a beloved Southern comfort dish that has deep roots in Atlanta's food scene. While its origins are often debated, the dish likely traces back to the late-night menus of Harlem's jazz clubs in the 1930s, where they combined the heartiness of fried chicken with the sweetness of waffles. The sweet-and-savory dish eventually made its way to the South, becoming a regional favorite. This recipe recreates Southern fried chicken and waffles in a mini sandwich for appetizer portions.

BONELESS FRIED CHICKEN

5 cups (1.2 L) buttermilk

¼ cup (60 ml) favorite hot sauce (I like Crystal)

10 medium-size boneless, skinless chicken thighs

4 cups (500 g) all-purpose flour

⅓ cup (45 g) cornstarch

2 tablespoons paprika

1 tablespoon garlic powder

2 tablespoons onion powder

1 tablespoon salt

1 tablespoon black pepper

½ teaspoon cayenne pepper

2 teaspoons baking powder

Vegetable oil, for frying

HOT HONEY DRIZZLE

1¼ cups (300 ml) honey

2 tablespoons favorite hot sauce (I like Crystal)

1 teaspoon cayenne pepper

1 tablespoon butter

WAFFLES

Nonstick cooking spray or melted butter

Buttermilk waffle mix of choice (I like Krusteaz)

1 To make the boneless fried chicken: In a large bowl, combine the buttermilk and ¼ cup (60 ml) hot sauce. Cut each chicken thigh in half, creating 20 boneless portions, and place them in the marinade. Cover and refrigerate for at least 4 hours, or overnight for extra flavor.

2 In a separate bowl, mix the flour, cornstarch, paprika, garlic powder, onion powder, salt, black pepper, ½ teaspoon cayenne pepper, and baking powder.

3 Heat about 1 to 2 inches (2.5 to 5 cm) of vegetable oil in a large pot or skillet to 350°F (175°C). Remove the chicken pieces from the marinade and dredge them in the seasoned flour mixture, shaking off the excess.

4 Carefully fry the chicken, in batches, for 10 to 12 minutes, flipping halfway through, until golden brown and the internal temperature reaches 165°F (75°C). Drain the fried chicken on a paper towel–lined cookie tray.

5 While the chicken is frying, make the hot honey drizzle: Combine the honey, hot sauce, 1 teaspoon cayenne pepper, and butter in a small saucepan. Warm over low heat, stirring until the butter melts and the mixture is smooth. Remove from the heat.

6 To make the waffles: Preheat a waffle iron and lightly coat it with nonstick spray or melted butter. Follow the directions on the waffle mix package to make enough batter for 10 waffles. Pour batter onto the preheated waffle iron and cook according to the manufacturer's instructions until golden and crisp, 3 to 4 minutes per waffle. Once cooked, cut each waffle into quarters.

7 To assemble the sandwiches: For each sandwich, place a fried chicken piece between 2 waffle quarters. Insert a toothpick through the mini waffle sandwich to hold it together, if desired, and place it on a large platter. Drizzle each sandwich with hot honey before serving.

Shrimp and Grits

PREP TIME: 20 minutes

COOK TIME: 40 minutes

YIELD: 15 servings

GRITS

6 cups (1.4 L) water

6 cups (1.4 L) chicken broth

3 cups (510 g) white stone-ground grits (see Extra Point)

3 cups (720 ml) heavy cream

3 cups (345 g) shredded sharp cheddar cheese

1½ teaspoons salt, or to taste

1 teaspoon black pepper, or to taste

6 tablespoons unsalted butter

SHRIMP

12 slices thick-cut bacon, diced medium

1 large red bell pepper, stem and seeds removed and diced small

2 large shallots, minced

2 medium plum tomatoes, diced small

6 cloves garlic, minced

3 pounds (1.4 kg) large (31/40) shrimp, peeled and deveined

1½ teaspoons paprika

1 teaspoon smoked paprika

1 teaspoon black pepper

1 teaspoon salt

1 cup (240 ml) low-sodium chicken broth

1 tablespoon favorite hot sauce

3 tablespoons fresh lemon juice

FOR GARNISHING

3 tablespoons minced fresh flat-leaf parsley

6 scallions, sliced

Shrimp and grits is a classic Southern dish with roots in coastal communities, where fresh shrimp is abundant and grits are a staple. Originally a simple fisherman's breakfast in South Carolina's Lowcountry, the dish evolved over time and gained popularity across the South, becoming a beloved comfort food. Today, shrimp and grits is often elevated with creamy, cheese-infused grits and shrimp cooked in a savory sauce with bacon, garlic, and spices, often topped with green onions or served with a side of collard greens. In Atlanta, this dish is a favorite at spots like Mary Mac's Tea Room, which offers a traditional approach with stone-ground cheesy grits and succulent shrimp sautéed in a flavorful sauce.

1 To make the grits: In a large pot, bring the water and 6 cups (1.4 L) chicken broth to a boil over high heat. Gradually stir in the grits, reduce the heat to low, and cook, stirring occasionally, for 20 to 25 minutes, until the grits are tender and thickened.

2 Stir in the cream, cheese, 1½ teaspoons salt, black pepper, and butter. Adjust seasoning to taste. Cover and keep warm.

3 To make the shrimp: In a large skillet, cook the diced bacon over medium heat until crispy, 8 to 10 minutes. Transfer to a paper towel–lined plate. Drain all but 2 to 3 tablespoons of the bacon drippings from the skillet.

4 To the same skillet, add the bell pepper and shallots and cook, stirring often, for 4 to 5 minutes, until softened. Add the tomatoes and cook over medium heat for another 2 minutes. Add the garlic and cook for an additional minute.

5 Season the shrimp with the paprika, smoked paprika, black pepper, and 1 teaspoon salt. Add the shrimp to the skillet and cook for 1 to 2 minutes per side, until pink and opaque. Pour in the 1 cup (240 ml) chicken broth, hot sauce, and lemon juice, scraping up any browned bits from the bottom of the pan with a wooden spoon. Let the sauce simmer over medium-high heat for 60 to 90 seconds to thicken slightly. Stir in the crispy bacon.

6 Spoon the warm, cheesy grits onto plates or into bowls. Top each serving with a generous portion of shrimp and sauce. Garnish with the minced parsley and sliced scallions.

EXTRA POINT

Make sure you aren't using instant grits, just plain ones; I recommend Quaker brand.

CAROLINA PANTHERS

Biscuits with Fried Green Tomatoes

PREP TIME: 30 minutes

COOK TIME: 30 minutes

YIELD: 15 sandwiches

Sweet potato biscuits and fried green tomatoes are cherished Southern comfort foods, particularly in Charlotte, North Carolina. Sweet potato biscuits, made with rich, creamy mashed sweet potatoes and flour, offer a slightly sweet and savory flavor, while fried green tomatoes, typically coated in cornmeal and fried until golden, are deliciously tart.

SWEET POTATO BISCUITS

2 cups (250 g) all-purpose flour

¼ cup (50 g) sugar

1 tablespoon baking powder

½ teaspoon baking soda

½ teaspoon salt

½ cup (115 g, or 1 stick) cold unsalted butter, placed in freezer for 10 minutes

1 (15-ounce, or 425-gram) can sweet potatoes in syrup, drained (reserve 2 tablespoons of the syrup for the Herb Cream Cheese Spread)

½ cup (120 ml) buttermilk

⅛ teaspoon vanilla extract

FRIED GREEN TOMATOES

1 cup (240 ml) buttermilk

1 cup (180 g) cornmeal

1 cup (125 g) all-purpose flour, plus more for dusting

1 teaspoon salt

1 teaspoon black pepper

5 small green tomatoes (3 to 4 inches, or 7.5 to 10 cm, in diameter; see Extra Point), sliced into ¼-inch-thick (6 mm) rounds (about 15 slices)

Vegetable oil, for frying

HERB CREAM CHEESE SPREAD

8 ounces (227 g) cream cheese, softened

2 tablespoons chopped fresh flat-leaf parsley

1 tablespoon chopped fresh chives

Salt and black pepper

1. **To make the sweet potato biscuits:** Preheat the oven to 425°F (220°C) and line a baking sheet with parchment paper.

2. In a large bowl, whisk together the flour, sugar, baking powder, baking soda, and ½ teaspoon salt. Using a box grater, grate the frozen butter into the bowl and cut it into the flour mixture with a pastry cutter or large fork. The mixture should resemble large crumbs.

3. In a small bowl, mash the sweet potatoes with a fork. Stir the mashed sweet potatoes, ½ cup (120 ml) buttermilk, and vanilla extract into the flour mixture until just combined. Do not overmix!

4. Turn out the dough onto a floured surface and gently pat it into a 1-inch-thick (2.5 cm) rectangle. Cut it into small circles (about 2 inches, or 5 cm, in diameter) using a biscuit cutter. Place the biscuits on the prepared baking sheet.

5. Bake for 12 to 15 minutes, until golden brown. Keep warm by covering with a towel.

6. **Meanwhile, make the fried green tomatoes:** Set up a dredging station with one bowl with the 1 cup (240 ml) buttermilk and another bowl with a mix of the cornmeal, flour, 1 teaspoon salt, and 1 teaspoon pepper. Dip each tomato slice in the buttermilk, allowing excess to drip off, then coat it in the cornmeal mixture.

7. Heat about ½ inch (13 mm) of vegetable oil in a large skillet over medium-high heat. When the oil is hot, carefully fry the tomatoes, in batches, for 2 to 3 minutes per side, until golden brown and crispy. Transfer to a paper towel–lined plate.

8. **To make the herb cream cheese spread:** In a small bowl, combine the softened cream cheese and reserved sweet potato syrup. Mix in the parsley and chives and season with salt and pepper to taste. Blend until smooth and well combined.

9. **To assemble the sandwiches:** Split the biscuits in half horizontally. Spread a generous amount of herb cream cheese on the bottom halves, then top each one with a tomato and the remaining biscuit half. Serve the sandwiches on a large platter.

EXTRA POINT

If you cannot find green tomatoes, you can use tomatillos or even just very firm red tomatoes.

Carolina Pulled Pork Sandwiches with Slaw

PREP TIME: 20 minutes

COOK TIME: 6 to 12 hours

YIELD: 14 sandwiches

Carolina pulled pork sandwiches are a beloved regional specialty in Charlotte, North Carolina, deeply rooted in the Carolinas' barbecue traditions. Typically, the dish features slow-smoked pork seasoned with a tangy vinegar-based sauce, a hallmark of Eastern North Carolina barbecue. The tender pork is shredded and served on a soft bun and often paired with a crisp slaw for a perfect balance of smoky and tangy flavors.

PULLED PORK

2 tablespoons brown sugar

2 tablespoons paprika

1 tablespoon garlic powder

1 tablespoon onion powder

1 tablespoon salt

1 teaspoon black pepper

1 teaspoon cayenne pepper

6 pounds (2.7 kg) boneless pork shoulder (or pork butt)

1 cup (240 ml) apple cider vinegar

¼ cup (60 ml) Worcestershire sauce

¼ cup (60 ml) yellow mustard

SLAW

2 (14-ounce, or 397-g) packages cabbage slaw mix

1 cup (240 ml) mayonnaise

2 tablespoons apple cider vinegar

1 tablespoon sugar

1 teaspoon salt

½ teaspoon black pepper

CAROLINA VINEGAR SAUCE

1 cup (240 ml) apple cider vinegar

2 tablespoons brown sugar

1 tablespoon Worcestershire sauce

1 teaspoon black pepper

1 teaspoon salt

½ teaspoon red pepper flakes

SANDWICHES

14 potato hamburger buns

Pickles, for serving

Potato chips, for serving

1 To make the pulled pork: In a small bowl, mix the brown sugar, paprika, garlic powder, onion powder, 1 tablespoon salt, 1 teaspoon black pepper, and cayenne pepper until well combined. Rub this spice mixture all over the pork shoulder.

2 In a medium bowl, mix the vinegar, Worcestershire sauce, and yellow mustard until well combined.

3 If using a slow cooker, add the vinegar mixture over the top of the pork. Cook on low for 10 to 12 hours, until the pork is pulled apart and tender. If using a smoker, smoke at 225 to 250°F (110 to 120°C) for 6 to 8 hours, basting occasionally with the vinegar mixture, until tender. Remove the pork from the cooker or smoker and let rest for 15 to 20 minutes. Use two large forks to shred the meat, being careful not to break up the strands too much.

4 To make the slaw: At least 30 minutes before serving (so that the dressing can soften the cabbage and carrots), put the coleslaw mix into a large bowl. In a separate bowl, whisk together the mayonnaise, vinegar, sugar, 1 teaspoon salt, and ½ teaspoon black pepper. Pour the dressing over the coleslaw mix, then toss to combine. Refrigerate until serving.

5 To make the Carolina vinegar sauce: Combine all the sauce ingredients in a medium saucepan. Heat over medium heat, stirring until the sugar dissolves. Bring to a simmer and let cook for 5 to 10 minutes. Remove from the heat and let cool.

6 To assemble the sandwiches: Place a generous portion of the pork on the bottom of a potato bun, drizzling the sauce over the pork. Top the pork with a scoop of slaw and the other half of the bun. Serve the sandwiches on individual plates with pickles and potato chips.

TWO-POINT CONVERSION

You can cook the pork overnight in the slow cooker, starting 10 to 12 hours or the day before you are going to serve it.

You can also smoke the pork the day before. It can be pulled when finished and then reheated for the sandwiches on game day. Always remember to reheat cooked meats, covered, to a temperature of 165°F (75°C).

NEW ORLEANS SAINTS

Mini Fried Shrimp Po'Boys

PREP TIME: 25 minutes

COOK TIME: 15 minutes

YIELD: 18 mini po'boys

FRIED SHRIMP

3 pounds (1.4 kg) medium (31/40) shrimp, peeled and deveined

2 cups (480 ml) buttermilk

2 cups (360 g) cornmeal

1 cup (125 g) all-purpose flour

1½ teaspoons paprika

1½ teaspoons garlic powder

1 teaspoon cayenne pepper

2 teaspoons salt

1 teaspoon black pepper

Vegetable oil, for frying

REMOULADE SAUCE

1½ cups (360 ml) mayonnaise

2½ tablespoons Dijon mustard

1½ tablespoons ketchup

2½ tablespoons pickle relish

2 tablespoons favorite hot sauce (I like Crystal)

2 teaspoons capers, drained and chopped fine

2 tablespoons fresh lemon juice

2 cloves garlic, minced

½ teaspoon paprika

Salt and black pepper

PO'BOY SANDWICHES

18 crusty torpedo dinner rolls (or nine 4-inch (10 cm) baguettes cut in half)

2 cups (110 g) shredded lettuce

3 medium tomatoes, thinly sliced

Potato chips, for serving

Favorite hot sauce, for serving

Dill pickle slices, for serving

Fried shrimp po'boys are an iconic New Orleans dish, steeped in the rich culinary history of the city. Originating during the 1929 streetcar strike, the sandwich was served to striking workers—"poor boys" (hence the name)—by Bennie and Clovis Martin, former streetcar workers turned restaurant owners. The traditional po'boy consists of crispy fried shrimp nestled in a French bread loaf with a crisp exterior and soft interior, typically dressed with lettuce, tomato, pickles, and mayonnaise and often accompanied with a zesty remoulade and hot sauce for extra flavor. In New Orleans, Domilise's Po-Boy and Bar has been serving po'boys since the 1920s, offering a perfectly fried shrimp po'boy with fresh toppings. At Parkway Bakery and Tavern, a historic spot dating back to 1911, the shrimp po'boy is served fully dressed, along with sides like fries or potato salad.

1 To make the fried shrimp: In a large bowl, combine the shrimp and buttermilk. In another bowl, mix the cornmeal, flour, 1½ teaspoons paprika, garlic powder, cayenne pepper, 2 teaspoons salt, and 1 teaspoon black pepper until well combined.

2 Line a baking sheet with parchment paper. Remove the shrimp from the buttermilk, letting excess drip off, then dredge each shrimp in the cornmeal mixture until fully coated, laying each coated shrimp flat on the prepared baking sheet, avoiding overlap.

3 Heat about 2 inches (5 cm) of vegetable oil in a deep, wide pan over medium-high heat. When the oil is hot. Carefully fry the shrimp, in batches, for 2 to 3 minutes, until golden brown and crispy. Transfer to a paper towel–lined plate to drain, then place the crispy shrimp on a large platter. Cover lightly with foil and keep warm.

4 To make the remoulade sauce: In a medium bowl, combine the mayonnaise, mustard, ketchup, relish, hot sauce, capers, lemon juice, minced garlic, and ½ teaspoon paprika. Season with salt and black pepper to taste and mix well (there will be small bits of pickle, caper, and garlic). Transfer to a serving bowl.

5 To assemble the sandwiches: Slice the dinner rolls in half horizontally and place in a deep bowl. Place the shredded lettuce and tomato slices on a platter next to the rolls, along with the bowl of remoulade and platter of fried shrimp. Allow the guests to assemble their mini sandwiches in the following order: put 1 tablespoon of remoulade on the roll, add 2 or 3 fried shrimp, and top with shredded lettuce and a slice of tomato. Serve with potato chips, hot sauce, and pickles on a large platter. Drizzle each sandwich with more remoulade sauce before serving.

NEW ORLEANS SAINTS

Chicken and Andouille Sausage Gumbo

PREP TIME: 25 minutes

COOK TIME: 2 to 3 hours

YIELD: 12 servings

GUMBO

1 cup (225 g, or 2 sticks) unsalted butter

1 cup (125 g) all-purpose flour

2 large onions, diced small

2 bell peppers, diced medium

4 ribs celery, diced medium

4 cloves garlic, minced

1 pound (454 g) andouille sausage, sliced into ¼-inch (6 mm) rounds

1½ pounds (680 g) boneless, skinless chicken thighs, cut into bite-size pieces

1½ tablespoons creole seasoning

1 tablespoon smoked paprika

¼ teaspoon cayenne pepper

8 cups (1.9 ml) low-sodium chicken broth

2 bay leaves

1½ teaspoons Worcestershire sauce

1 tablespoon favorite hot sauce (I use Tabasco or Louisiana)

1½ cups (230 g) sliced (¼ inch, or 6 mm, thick) fresh or frozen okra

1 teaspoon gumbo filé powder (or substitute 1 cup, or 155 g, sliced okra) (optional)

Salt and black pepper

FOR SERVING AND GARNISHING

8 cups (1.6 kg) cooked long-grain white rice

12 (2-inch, or 5-cm) slices crusty French bread or corn bread

Thinly sliced scallions

Chicken and andouille sausage gumbo is a cornerstone of New Orleans cuisine, embodying the city's diverse cultural roots. Gumbo combines French, African, and Native American influences, with its name likely derived from the West African word for okra, *gombo*. The dish gained prominence in the eighteenth century and is known for its dark roux, which forms the foundation of many versions. Chicken and andouille sausage, a spicy smoked pork sausage, are common ingredients, along with the "holy trinity" of Cajun cooking—onions, bell peppers, and celery. The stew is slow-cooked and seasoned with creole spices and often thickened with either filé powder (ground sassafras leaves) or okra. Two renowned spots to savor gumbo in New Orleans include Gumbo Shop, a longtime favorite in the French Quarter, and Mother's Restaurant, known for serving up hearty portions of this Southern classic.

1 In a large, heavy-bottom pot or Dutch oven, melt the butter over medium heat. Gradually whisk in the flour to create the roux. Cook for 20 to 25 minutes, stirring constantly, until the roux becomes a deep, dark brown. Keep stirring to avoid burning; do not leave the roux or it will burn.

2 Add the onions, bell peppers, and celery to the roux. Cook over medium-high heat for for 5 to 7 minutes, stirring often, until the vegetables begin to soften. Add the garlic and cook for another 2 minutes. Stir in the sausage and cook for 4 to 5 minutes, until the sausage starts to brown.

3 Stir in the chicken and cook for 5 to 7 minutes to brown slightly. Add the creole seasoning, smoked paprika, and cayenne pepper. Stir to combine. Gradually pour in the chicken broth while stirring. Add the bay leaves, Worcestershire sauce, and hot sauce. Bring the mixture to a boil, then reduce the heat to low and let simmer, uncovered, for 1½ to 2 hours, stirring occasionally.

4 About 30 minutes before the gumbo is done, add the okra. This helps thicken the gumbo naturally. If using filé powder, add it right at the end, after removing the gumbo from heat. (If you don't have filé powder, adding extra okra can help thicken the dish in its place.)

5 Taste the gumbo and adjust the seasoning as needed, adding more salt, black pepper, and/or hot sauce to taste.

6 Place a scoop of rice in each serving bowl and ladle the gumbo over the rice. Serve with crusty French bread or corn bread to soak up the rich, flavorful sauce. Garnish the gumbo with sliced scallions.

Deviled Crab Croquettes

PREP TIME: 30 minutes, plus 1 hour chilling

COOK TIME: 15 minutes

YIELD: 15 croquettes

CROQUETTES

2 tablespoons unsalted butter

2 tablespoons olive oil

1 small onion, finely chopped

1 small green bell pepper, finely chopped

2 cloves garlic, minced

2 pounds (907 g) lump crabmeat, picked clean of any shells

½ cup (120 ml) mayonnaise

2 tablespoons Dijon mustard

2 tablespoons Worcestershire sauce

2 tablespoons favorite hot sauce

2 teaspoons Old Bay Seasoning

½ teaspoon cayenne pepper

1 teaspoon paprika

2 tablespoons chopped fresh flat-leaf parsley

1 cup (100 g) bread crumbs

2 large eggs, beaten

2 tablespoons fresh lemon juice

Salt and black pepper

Vegetable oil, for frying

COATING

1 cup (125 g) all-purpose flour

2 large eggs, beaten

2 cups (200 g) bread crumbs

1 teaspoon Old Bay Seasoning

FOR SERVING

Lemon wedges

Tartar sauce, cocktail sauce, or spicy mayonnaise

Deviled crab croquettes are a beloved regional dish in Tampa Bay, with deep roots in the area's Cuban and Spanish culinary traditions. The dish originated in the early 1900s, when Tampa's Ybor City became home to thousands of Cuban immigrants working in the cigar industry. Workers needed portable, affordable meals, and the deviled crab croquette was born. The croquettes are traditionally seasoned with paprika, garlic, and sometimes hot sauce, giving them their signature "deviled" flavor. Today, you can still find these croquettes served at iconic Tampa eateries like Columbia Restaurant, Florida's oldest restaurant in Ybor City.

1 To make the croquettes: In a medium skillet, heat the butter and olive oil over medium heat. Add the onion, bell pepper, and garlic and cook, stirring often, for 5 to 7 minutes, until the onion is softened and slightly translucent. Remove from the heat and let cool to room temperature, about 8 minutes.

2 In a large bowl, combine the crabmeat, cooked vegetables, mayonnaise, mustard, Worcestershire sauce, hot sauce, 2 teaspoons Old Bay, cayenne pepper, paprika, parsley, 1 cup (100 g) bread crumbs, and beaten eggs. Add the lemon juice, then the salt and black pepper to taste. Gently mix the ingredients with a rubber spatula, being careful not to break up the crabmeat too much. The mixture should hold together when spooned but still be soft and moist.

3 Portion ¼ cup (60 g) of the crab mixture per croquette (this is the perfect size for an appetizer; the uniform size will ensure even cooking). Form the crab mixture into ovals (2 inches, or 5 cm, long and 1 inch, or 2.5 cm, thick) for 15 croquettes. Place the croquettes on a baking sheet and refrigerate for at least 1 hour to firm up.

4 To make the coating: Set up a breading station with the flour in one shallow dish, the beaten eggs in another shallow dish, and the 2 cups (200 g) bread crumbs mixed with the 1 teaspoon Old Bay in a third one. First coat each croquette in the flour, then dip it in the egg mixture, and finally coat it with the bread crumbs. Ensure each croquette is fully covered with bread crumbs for a crispy coating and that they are the same size and shape, once again, for even cooking.

5 Heat about 1 inch (2.5 cm) of vegetable oil in a large skillet over medium-high heat until it reaches 350°F (175°C). Carefully fry the croquettes, in batches, being careful not to overcrowd the pan. Cook for 3 to 4 minutes on each side, until golden brown and crispy. Transfer the croquettes to a paper towel-lined plate.

6 Serve the croquettes hot on a large platter with lemon wedges for squeezing and dipping sauce of choice.

TAMPA BAY BUCCANEERS

Blackened Fish Sandwiches

PREP TIME: 20 minutes

COOK TIME: 15 minutes

YIELD: 10 sandwiches

A blackened grouper sandwich is a Tampa Bay favorite, showcasing the area's love for fresh seafood and bold flavors. Grouper, a mild yet meaty fish native to the Gulf of Mexico, is seasoned with a blend of Cajun spices and then seared in a hot cast-iron skillet to achieve its signature blackened crust. The sandwich is typically served on a toasted bun with toppings like lettuce, tomato, and a tangy remoulade or tartar sauce.

BLACKENED FISH

1½ tablespoons paprika

2 teaspoons garlic powder

2 teaspoons onion powder

2 teaspoons dried thyme

2 teaspoons dried oregano

1 teaspoon cayenne pepper

2 teaspoons black pepper

2 teaspoons salt

2½ pounds (1.1 kg) fresh grouper fillets (ten 4-ounce, or 113-g, pieces; see Extra Point)

2½ tablespoons olive oil

2½ tablespoons butter, divided

SAUCE

¾ cup (180 ml) mayonnaise

3 tablespoons Dijon mustard

3 tablespoons fresh lemon juice

SANDWICHES

10 brioche or potato hamburger buns, sliced in half horizontally and toasted

10 leaves lettuce (I use leaf or butter lettuce)

2 large tomatoes, sliced ¼ inch (6 mm) thick

10 (¼-inch-thick, or 6-mm-thick) slices red onion

20 dill pickle slices

French fries, potato chips, and/or coleslaw, for serving

1 To make the blackened fish: In a small bowl, mix the paprika, garlic powder, onion powder, thyme, oregano, cayenne pepper, black pepper, and salt until well combined.

2 Pat the fish fillets dry with a paper towel. Brush each fillet lightly with olive oil, then generously coat both sides with the seasoning mixture.

3 Heat a large cast-iron skillet over medium-high heat. Add 1 tablespoon of the butter and allow it to melt. Once the skillet is hot, cook the fillets, in batches, for 3 to 4 minutes per side, until blackened and cooked through (internal temperature should reach 145°F, or 63°C). Add more butter to the skillet as needed for each batch. Remove from the heat.

4 To make the sauce: In a small bowl, whisk together the mayonnaise, mustard, and lemon juice.

5 To assemble the sandwiches: Spread 1 tablespoon of the sauce on each half of a toasted bun. Place a fish fillet on the bottom half of each bun and top with lettuce, tomato, red onion, and pickles. Top with the remaining half of the bun. Serve the sandwiches immediately with french fries, potato chips, and/or coleslaw.

EXTRA POINT

If you can't find grouper, mahi-mahi and cod are excellent substitutes due to their firm texture and ability to hold up well to blackening.

★ NFC ★ EAST

DALLAS COWBOYS

**CHICKEN-FRIED STEAK BITES
WITH GRAVY 131**

TEXAS RED CHILI 132

NEW YORK GIANTS

DISCO FRIES 135

CHOPPED CHEESE SANDWICHES 136

PHILADELPHIA EAGLES

CHEESESTEAK EGG ROLLS 139

ROAST PORK SANDWICHES 140

WASHINGTON COMMANDERS

HALF-SMOKE BITES 143

CHICKEN WINGS WITH MUMBO SAUCE 144

DALLAS COWBOYS

Chicken-Fried Steak Bites with Gravy

PREP TIME: 20 minutes, plus 30 minutes marinating

COOK TIME: 20 minutes

YIELD: 24 bites

Chicken-fried steak is a Texas classic with deep roots in Southern and cowboy cuisine that are particularly cherished in Dallas. This comfort dish features a tenderized beef steak (often round steak or cube steak) that is coated in buttermilk, dredged in seasoned flour, and then fried to crispy perfection—similar to how fried chicken is prepared, hence the name. In and around Dallas, chicken-fried steak is a menu staple at local institutions like Babe's Chicken Dinner House, where the dish is served with homestyle sides and a welcoming atmosphere.

CHICKEN FRIED STEAK BITES

3 pounds (1.4 kg) cube steak, cut into 24 (2-ounce, or 57-g) pieces

1 cup (240 ml) buttermilk

1 cup (125 g) all-purpose flour

1 teaspoon paprika

1 teaspoon garlic powder

1 teaspoon onion powder

1 teaspoon salt

½ teaspoon black pepper

Vegetable oil, for frying

CREAMY GRAVY

2 tablespoons butter

2 tablespoons all-purpose flour

½ cup (120 ml) chicken stock

1 cup (240 ml) milk

½ teaspoon garlic powder

½ teaspoon onion powder

Salt and black pepper

2 tablespoons finely chopped fresh flat-leaf parsley

1 To make the chicken-fried steak bites: Place the steak pieces in a large bowl and pour buttermilk over them. Cover and refrigerate for at least 30 minutes to tenderize the meat.

2 In a shallow dish, mix the flour, paprika, 1 teaspoon garlic powder, 1 teaspoon onion powder, 1 teaspoon salt, and ½ teaspoon pepper until well combined. Remove the steak from the buttermilk, allowing any excess to drip off. Dredge each piece in the seasoned flour mixture, pressing lightly to adhere. Set aside on a platter, being careful not to overlap the pieces.

3 In a large skillet, heat about ½ inch (13 mm) of oil over medium-high heat until hot (about 350°F, or 175°C). Carefully add the breaded steak pieces, in batches, making sure not to overcrowd the pan. Fry for 3 to 4 minutes on each side, until golden brown and crispy. Transfer to a paper towel–lined plate. Keep warm.

4 To make the creamy gravy: After frying the steak, carefully drain the oil from the skillet, leaving behind any browned bits and about 1 teaspoon of the oil. Add the butter to the pan and melt over medium heat. Whisk in the flour, stirring constantly for 1 to 2 minutes, until light golden brown and combined with the crispy bits.

5 Gradually whisk in the chicken stock, followed by the milk, stirring constantly to avoid lumps. Add the ½ teaspoon garlic powder and ½ teaspoon onion powder and season with salt and pepper to taste. Continue whisking until the gravy thickens to the desired consistency, 3 to 4 minutes.

6 Arrange the chicken-fried steak bites on a platter and top with the chopped parsley. Drizzle with the creamy gravy or serve the gravy on the side for dipping.

DALLAS COWBOYS

Texas Red Chili

PREP TIME: 30 minutes

COOK TIME: 2 hours
30 minutes to 3 hours

YIELD: 15 servings

CHILI

6 dried ancho chili peppers

6 dried guajillo chili peppers

4 tablespoons (60 ml) vegetable oil, divided

5 pounds (2.3 kg) beef chuck roast, cut into ½-inch (13 mm) cubes

2 medium yellow onions, finely chopped

10 cloves garlic, minced

2 tablespoons ground cumin

2 tablespoons paprika

2 tablespoons dried Mexican oregano

1 tablespoon chili powder

1 tablespoon black pepper

2 teaspoons kosher salt, or to taste

2 teaspoons cayenne pepper (optional)

4 cups (960 ml) beef broth

1 tablespoon masa harina or Wondra flour (optional)

TOPPINGS

Small-diced white onion

Shredded cheddar cheese

Sour cream

Sliced jalapeños

FOR SERVING

Corn bread

Texas red is a hearty, no-bean chili made with chunks of beef and a rich blend of chili peppers and spices. Unlike other chili varieties, Texas red steers clear of tomatoes and beans, focusing instead on the smoky, savory heat of dried chili peppers, typically ancho or guajillo, and the natural richness of the meat. This dish has been a staple in Texas since the cattle-driving days of the 1800s, when cowboys needed a simple yet filling meal that could be prepared on the range.

1 Remove the stems and seeds from the ancho and guajillo chili peppers. Heat a dry skillet over medium heat and toast the chilies until fragrant, about 2 minutes per side. Be careful not to burn them. Place the toasted chilies in a bowl and cover them with boiling water. Let them soak for 15 to 20 minutes, until softened. Drain, reserving the soaking water, and transfer to a blender. Add a little of the soaking water and blend into a smooth paste.

2 In a large Dutch oven, heat 2 tablespoons of the vegetable oil over medium-high heat. Working in batches, brown the cubed beef on all sides, 4 to 5 minutes per batch. Remove the meat from the pot.

3 In the same pot, reduce the heat to medium, add the remaining 2 tablespoons vegetable oil and cook the onions, stirring often, until softened and translucent, 5 to 6 minutes. Add the garlic and cook for an additional minute. Stir in the cumin, paprika, oregano, chili powder, black pepper, salt, and cayenne pepper (if using). Let the spices toast for 1 to 2 minutes, until fragrant.

4 Return the browned beef to the pot, then pour in the broth and the chili pepper paste. Bring the mixture to a simmer over medium-high heat, then reduce the heat to low, cover the pot, and let cook for 2 hours to 2 hours and 30 minutes, stirring occasionally, until the beef is tender. If the chili gets too thick, add water or broth as needed to maintain the desired consistency.

5 Taste the chili and adjust the salt, black pepper, and/or heat with more cayenne (if using). For a thicker consistency, stir in the masa harina or Wondra flour mixed with a little water and let the chili simmer for another 10 minutes.

6 Ladle the chili into bowls and set out the optional toppings (onions, cheese, sour cream, and/or jalapeños) in bowls for choosing. Serve with corn bread.

Disco Fries

PREP TIME: 10 minutes

COOK TIME: 30 minutes

YIELD: 15 servings

Disco fries, known for its late-night appeal and diner roots, is a regional comfort-food favorite in New York and Northern New Jersey. The dish consists of a generous portion of french fries topped with melted mozzarella cheese and smothered in a rich brown gravy. Often compared to the Canadian poutine, disco fries have their own distinct identity, popularized in the 1970s when they became a staple for club-goers looking for a hearty snack after a night of drinking and dancing.

FRIES

About 4 to 6 cups (1 to 1.4 L) vegetable oil or oil of choice, for frying (optional)

4 pounds (1.8 kg) frozen thick-cut french fries

Salt

GRAVY

½ small onion, diced large

1 small carrot, diced large

1 rib celery, diced large

3 cloves garlic, smashed with the flat of a knife

6 peppercorns

1 bay leaf

3 cups (720 ml) beef stock or broth

3 tablespoons unsalted butter

3 tablespoons all-purpose flour

1½ teaspoons Worcestershire sauce

Salt and black pepper

FOR FINISHING

3 cups (330 g) shredded mozzarella cheese

2 cups (230 g) shredded white cheddar cheese

1   **To make the fries:** If frying, heat the oil in a deep fryer or large, heavy-bottomed pot to 350°F (175°C). Carefully fry the frozen fries, in batches, until golden brown and crispy, 5 to 7 minutes. Drain on paper towels and keep hot in a metal tray. Salt to taste. If air-frying, preheat the air fryer to 400°F (205°C) for 5 minutes. Place the frozen fries in the air-fryer basket in a single layer (you may need to do this in batches). Cook for 15 to 20 minutes, shaking the basket halfway through, until golden and crispy. Salt to taste. Keep hot in a metal tray.

2   **To make the gravy:** Preheat the oven to 375°F (190°C). In a medium saucepan over medium-high heat, add the onion, carrot, celery, garlic, peppercorns, bay leaf, and beef stock. Bring to a simmer, then reduce the heat to medium-low and let cook for 10 minutes. Strain and reserve the beef stock and discard the vegetables and spices.

3   In the same saucepan, melt the butter over medium heat. Whisk in the flour to make a roux, cooking for 1 to 2 minutes for a golden gravy or 4 to 5 minutes for a darker gravy. Gradually whisk in the reserved beef stock and bring to a simmer. Add the Worcestershire sauce and continue to cook until thickened, 5 to 7 minutes, stirring often. Season with salt and pepper to taste. Keep the gravy hot.

4   **To finish:** Transfer the fries to a large, oven-safe serving platter. Evenly sprinkle the fries with the cheese. Place the platter in the oven and bake for 3 to 5 minutes, until the cheese is fully melted.

5   Remove the platter from the oven. Drizzle the gravy over the cheesy fries. Serve immediately with extra gravy.

NEW YORK GIANTS

Chopped Cheese Sandwiches

PREP TIME: 10 minutes

COOK TIME: 15 to 20 minutes

YIELD: 12 sandwiches

12 sub rolls

2 tablespoons vegetable oil

2 medium onions, finely chopped

4 pounds (1.8 kg) ground beef (80/20)

2 teaspoons garlic powder

2 teaspoons onion powder

Salt and black pepper

16 deli slices American cheese (or choice of cheese)

Mayonnaise

Ketchup (optional)

Shredded lettuce

Sliced tomatoes

Potato chips, for serving

The chopped cheese, a beloved staple of New York's deli and bodega scene that originated at a bodega in East Harlem, is quintessential urban comfort food. This sandwich typically consists of ground beef, sautéed onions, and melted cheese, all served on a sub roll. The dish's simplicity and satisfying flavor have made it a favorite among New Yorkers from all walks of life, often enjoyed as a quick lunch or late-night snack. Often paired with a side of chips or a soda, the chopped cheese sandwich embodies the spirit of New York's diverse culinary landscape, reflecting the city's love for hearty, flavorful food.

1 Preheat the oven to 375°F (190°C). Slice the sub rolls in half horizontally and place on two large baking sheets. Lightly toast the rolls in the oven until golden brown, 2 to 4 minutes.

2 In a large, wide skillet or deep pot, heat the vegetable oil over medium heat (this can also be done on a large griddle, like a Blackstone). Add the onions, cooking, stirring often, until golden brown, 5 to 7 minutes. Add the ground beef, breaking it up with a rubber spatula. Season with the garlic powder, onion powder and salt and pepper to taste. Cook until the beef is browned and fully cooked, 8 to 10 minutes.

3 Use the rubber spatula to chop the meat and onions together into smaller pieces. Mix well to ensure everything is evenly distributed. Reduce the heat to medium-low.

4 Layer 8 slices of the American cheese on the hot beef mixture. As it fully melts, chop the cheese into the beef mixture. Place the remaining 8 cheese slices on top and let it melt over the meat. Chop/mix the melted cheese into the beef until fully incorporated.

5 Divide the cheesy beef mixture into 12 (5-ounce, or 142 g) portions with a spatula.

6 Spread mayo evenly on the bottom halves of the toasted sub rolls. Evenly distribute the chopped cheese mixture portions among the rolls, using a metal spatula to scoop it onto the bottom half of each roll. Add ketchup (if using).

7 Top each sandwich with shredded lettuce and sliced tomatoes. Close the sandwiches with the top halves of the rolls and serve immediately with potato chips.

Cheesesteak Egg Rolls

PREP TIME: 30 minutes

COOK TIME: 25 minutes

YIELD: 24 egg rolls

CHEESESTEAK EGG ROLLS

2 tablespoons vegetable oil or butter

2 pounds (907 g) rib-eye steak, thinly sliced or chipped (or 2 pounds, or 907 g, frozen Philly cheesesteak product, like Steak-Eze)

2 large onions, finely chopped

2 green bell peppers, finely chopped

1 teaspoon garlic powder

1 teaspoon kosher salt

1 teaspoon black pepper

24 egg roll wrappers

2 cups (230 g) shredded provolone cheese (or Cheez Whiz)

1 large egg, beaten

About 4 cups (960 ml) vegetable or canola oil, for frying

SRIRACHA KETCHUP

1 cup (240 ml) ketchup

2 tablespoons sriracha, or to taste

Cheesesteak egg rolls are a modern twist on Philadelphia's iconic cheesesteak sandwich, blending the beloved flavors of thinly sliced beef, melted cheese, and sautéed onions into a crispy, bite-size appetizer. This fusion dish has become a popular option at bars, restaurants, and food trucks around the city. In Philadelphia, cheesesteak egg rolls are typically served at places like The Continental Mid-town, known for its upscale, globally inspired menu that incorporates local favorites. The rolls are often paired with dipping sauces like sriracha ketchup or cheese sauce, making them a perfect snack for both locals and visitors looking to enjoy a new take on a Philly classic.

1 To make the egg rolls: Heat the vegetable oil or butter in a large skillet over medium-high heat. If using fresh rib-eye steak, add it to the pan and cook for 4 to 5 minutes, until browned all over. If using a frozen product like Steak-Eze, cook according to the package instructions.

2 Add the onions and bell peppers and cook, stirring often, until softened, about 5 minutes. Season with the garlic powder, salt, and black pepper and cook for 2 more minutes. Remove from the heat and allow the mixture to cool slightly.

3 Place an egg roll wrapper on a clean surface with a corner facing you, like a diamond. Spoon 2 to 3 tablespoons of the steak mixture into the center of the wrapper, then top with about 1 tablespoon shredded provolone. Fold the bottom corner up over the filling, fold the sides inward, and roll tightly. Brush the top corner with some beaten egg to seal the egg roll. Repeat with the remaining wrappers and filling.

4 Heat the oil in a large, heavy-bottomed pot to 350°F (175°C). Carefully fry 3 or 4 egg rolls at a time for 3 to 4 minutes, until golden brown and crispy. Transfer to a paper towel–lined plate. Keep hot.

5 To make the sriracha ketchup: In a small bowl, mix the ketchup and sriracha until smooth.

6 Serve the cheesesteak egg rolls hot, arranged on a large platter with the sriracha ketchup in the center for dipping.

EXTRA POINT

These can be made in different ways with different vegetables or cheeses. Some places add peppers; others only use onions with the meat. Some places add both provolone and American cheese. It really is about preference and how you like your cheesesteak.

PHILADELPHIA EAGLES

Roast Pork Sandwiches

PREP TIME: 20 minutes, plus 2 hours chilling

COOK TIME: 4 hours 15 minutes

YIELD: 12 sandwiches (24 halves)

The roast pork sandwich can be traced back to the Italian American communities in South Philadelphia, where Italian immigrants sought to recreate the flavors of their homeland. The sandwich evolved from the Italian porchetta, a dish of seasoned, roasted whole pig, and was popularized in local delis and sandwich shops. The roast pork sandwich typically features slow-roasted seasoned pork sliced thin and served on a fresh Italian roll, often topped with sautéed broccoli rabe, sharp provolone cheese, and sliced long hot peppers for an extra kick. Two iconic establishments that serve this regional favorite are Tommy DiNic's in the Reading Terminal Market, known for its award-winning version, and John's Roast Pork in South Philadelphia, which has been serving up its famous sandwiches since 1930.

ROAST PORK

8 cloves garlic, minced

1½ tablespoons dried thyme

2 tablespoons dried oregano

1 tablespoon minced fresh rosemary

3 tablespoons minced fresh flat-leaf parsley

1 tablespoon kosher salt

1 tablespoon black pepper

2 tablespoons garlic powder

2 tablespoons onion powder

1 tablespoon red pepper flakes

4 pounds (1.8 kg) boneless pork shoulder

1 tablespoon olive oil

1 cup (240 ml) chicken broth

BROCCOLI RABE

3 tablespoons olive oil

6 cloves garlic, minced

2 heads broccoli rabe, trimmed and chopped

Salt and black pepper

SANDWICHES

12 Italian or hoagie rolls

12 thin deli slices sharp provolone cheese

12 long hot peppers, roasted or sautéed and thinly sliced, plus more for serving (optional)

1 **To make the roast pork:** In a small bowl, mix the 8 cloves minced garlic, thyme, oregano, rosemary, parsley, kosher salt, 1 tablespoon black pepper, garlic powder, onion powder, and red pepper flakes until well combined. Rub the seasoning mixture all over the pork shoulder. Place it in a large resealable plastic bag or wrap it tightly in plastic wrap and refrigerate for at least 2 hours, or overnight for best flavor.

2 Preheat the oven to 300°F (150°C). In a large Dutch oven, heat the 1 tablespoon olive oil over medium-high heat. Sear the pork on all sides until browned, 3 to 4 minutes per side. Add the chicken broth to the pan, cover it with a lid or aluminum foil, and transfer it to the oven. Roast for up to 4 hours, or until the pork is fork-tender and has an internal temperature between 180 and 185°F (82 to 85°C).

3 **While the pork is roasting, make the broccoli rabe:** Heat the 3 tablespoons olive oil in a large skillet over medium heat. Add the 6 cloves minced garlic and cook, stirring frequently, until fragrant, about 30 seconds. Add the broccoli rabe, season with salt and black pepper to taste, and cook, stirring often, for 5 to 7 minutes, until the broccoli rabe is tender. Set aside and keep warm.

4 When the pork is done, let it rest for about 15 minutes. Then remove it from the pan, keeping the juices warm on the stovetop, and thinly slice it using a very sharp knife (you can also shred it with two forks, if you prefer). Return the pork to its reserved juices to reheat and absorb the flavor.

5 **To assemble the sandwiches:** Cut the Italian rolls in half horizontally. On the bottom halves of the rolls, layer some sliced pork (with juices), a slice of cheese, and a generous serving of cooked broccoli rabe. If desired, for extra heat, add the sliced hot peppers. Top with the remaining roll halves. Cut the sandwiches in half.

6 Serve warm on a large platter with more hot peppers (if using).

Half-Smoke Bites

PREP TIME: 20 minutes

COOK TIME: 45 minutes

YIELD: 36 bites

CHILI TOPPING

1 pound (454 g) ground beef

½ small onion, finely chopped

2 cloves garlic, minced

2 tablespoons tomato paste

1 tablespoon yellow mustard

2 tablespoons chili powder

1 teaspoon ground cumin

1 teaspoon smoked paprika

½ teaspoon cayenne pepper (optional)

½ teaspoon black pepper

1 teaspoon salt, or to taste

1 tablespoon apple cider vinegar

1 teaspoon Worcestershire sauce

1 cup (240 ml) beef broth

½ cup (120 ml) water

HALF-SMOKE BITES

12 smoked beef hot links (I like Hillshire Farms)

12 hot dog buns (preferably split-top)

½ cup (120 ml) yellow mustard

2 cups (230 g) finely shredded cheddar cheese

1 medium white onion, finely chopped

The half-smoke is a quintessential Washington, DC, street food, beloved by locals for its bold, smoky flavor. Thought to have originated in the early twentieth century, the half-smoke is typically a pork and beef sausage, coarsely ground and smoked, offering a spicier and more robust flavor than a traditional hot dog. Its name is said to come from being half pork and half beef, and the "smoke" refers to its preparation method. Traditionally served grilled or split, it's often topped with chili, onions, and mustard, making it a hearty and satisfying meal. Two iconic places to enjoy a half-smoke in DC are Ben's Chili Bowl, a historic establishment known for its legendary chili-topped half-smokes, and Weenie Beenie, a local favorite for its no-frills take on the dish. The following recipe provides an appetizer-size portion of this DC favorite.

1 To make the chili topping: In a large skillet, cook the ground beef over medium heat until browned, breaking it into small pieces with a wooden spoon as it cooks. Drain any excess fat. Add the onion and garlic to the pan and cook, stirring often, until the onions soften, about 5 minutes.

2 Stir in the tomato paste, mustard, chili powder, cumin, smoked paprika, cayenne pepper (if using), black pepper, and salt and cook for 2 more minutes. Add the vinegar and Worcestershire sauce to deglaze the pan, scraping up any browned bits with a wooden spoon. Pour in the beef broth and water and stir well.

3 Let the chili simmer over low heat for 20 to 25 minutes, stirring occasionally, until it thickens. Adjust seasoning if necessary.

4 To make the half-smoke bites: Grill or pan-fry the hot links in a large skillet over medium-high heat until fully cooked and browned on all sides. Alternatively, they can be baked in the oven at 350°F (175°C) for 10 to 12 minutes.

5 Place each hot link into a hot dog bun. Slice each assembled hot dog into thirds, creating 36 smaller bites. Place all the bites together on a large serving platter.

6 Drizzle the yellow mustard over the hot link bites, then spoon the chili on top. Sprinkle the cheese and onions on top of the chili. Secure each bite with a toothpick for easy serving.

WASHINGTON COMMANDERS

Chicken Wings with Mumbo Sauce

PREP TIME: 20 minutes

COOK TIME: 30 minutes

YIELD: 15 servings

CHICKEN WINGS

2 cups (250 g) all-purpose flour

1 tablespoon garlic powder

1 tablespoon onion powder

1 tablespoon paprika

1 teaspoon kosher salt

1 teaspoon black pepper

30 whole chicken wings (drum, flat, and tip still joined together)

4 to 5 cups (1 to 1.2 L) vegetable oil, for frying

MUMBO SAUCE

1 cup (240 ml) ketchup

½ cup (120 ml) pineapple juice

¼ cup (60 ml) apple cider vinegar

¼ cup (50 g) sugar

¼ cup (60 ml) honey

¼ cup (60 ml) favorite hot sauce (I like Louisiana Hot Sauce)

1 tablespoon soy sauce

1 tablespoon Worcestershire sauce

1 teaspoon garlic powder

1 teaspoon onion powder

½ teaspoon paprika

FOR SERVING

Shoestring french fries

Chicken with mumbo sauce is a regional favorite in Washington, DC, known for its flavorful pairing of fried chicken wings and a unique, tangy-sweet sauce. Mumbo Sauce is typically made with a blend of ketchup, vinegar, sugar, hot sauce, and spices, creating a balance of sweetness, acidity, and mild heat. While its exact origins are debated, the sauce is believed to have emerged from DC's African American carryout food culture in the mid-twentieth century, and it quickly became a staple across the city. Two popular ways to find chicken with mumbo sauce are via Capital City Mambo Sauce, a brand that sells bottled versions of the sauce and serves it at local events, and at Henry's Soul Cafe, a long-standing establishment known for its soul food and authentic take on this regional favorite.

1 To make the chicken wings: In a large bowl, mix the flour, 1 tablespoon garlic powder, 1 tablespoon onion powder, 1 tablespoon paprika, salt, and pepper. Coat the chicken wings in the seasoned flour mixture, shaking off any excess.

2 Heat the vegetable oil in a large, heavy-bottomed pot or deep fryer to 350°F (175°C). Carefully fry the chicken wings, in batches, for 8 to 10 minutes, until golden brown and cooked through. Transfer to a paper towel–plate.

3 To make the Mumbo Sauce: In a medium saucepan, combine the ketchup, pineapple juice, vinegar, sugar, honey, hot sauce, soy sauce, Worcestershire sauce, 1 teaspoon garlic powder, 1 teaspoon onion powder, and ½ teaspoon paprika. Cook, stirring occasionally, over medium heat until the sugar dissolves and the sauce thickens slightly, 5 to 7 minutes. Taste and adjust seasoning as needed. Let the sauce cool slightly.

4 Toss the crispy fried chicken wings in the Mumbo Sauce and serve on a large platter with shoestring french fries. Alternatively, serve the wings on a large platter with the sauce for dipping and the fries.

★ NFC ★
WEST

ARIZONA CARDINALS

CHEESE CRISPS 149

SONORAN HOT DOGS 150

LOS ANGELES RAMS

SOFRITO CHICKEN FLAUTAS 153

FRENCH DIP SANDWICHES 154

SAN FRANCISCO 49ERS

AVOCADO SOURDOUGH TOASTS 157

MISSION BURRITOS 158

SEATTLE SEAHAWKS

SMOKED SALMON CHOWDER 161

TERIYAKI CHICKEN 162

Cheese Crisps

PREP TIME: 15 minutes

COOK TIME: 10 minutes

YIELD: 20 servings

1 tablespoon olive oil or nonstick cooking spray, for greasing (optional)

20 (6-inch, or 15-cm) flour or corn tortillas

5 cups (600 g) shredded cheddar or Monterey Jack cheese (or a blend)

1 cup (150 g) sliced roasted or fresh chili peppers, such as Anaheim or jalapeño

Chopped fresh cilantro, for serving

Diced tomatoes, for serving

Sour cream, for serving

The cheese crisp embodies the culinary spirit of Arizona and showcases the region's Mexican and Southwestern influences. This simple yet delightful creation consists of a tortilla topped with a generous layer of cheese, traditionally adorned with roasted or sliced chili peppers and then baked until crispy and bubbly. Its origins can be traced back to the mid-twentieth century, when it emerged from the local food scene as a tasty bar snack and appetizer. El Bravo in Phoenix is a popular spot known for its classic cheese crisp, featuring a perfectly baked tortilla and an ample layer of gooey cheese, often complemented by fresh toppings.

1 Preheat the oven to 450°F (230°C). Line two baking sheets with parchment paper or lightly grease them with olive oil or nonstick spray. Place 10 tortillas on each baking sheet, arranging them in a single layer.

2 Evenly sprinkle about ¼ cup (30 g) of cheese on each tortilla. Add a few slices of chili peppers on top of the cheese.

3 Bake for 8 to 10 minutes, until the cheese is melted and bubbly and the edges of the tortillas are crispy. If necessary, rotate the baking sheets halfway through for even cooking. Remove from the oven and let cool for 1 minute. Cut each cheese crisp into quarters or eighths for easy serving.

4 Serve warm on a large platter with the toppings (chopped cilantro, diced tomatoes, and sour cream) in bowls for choosing.

ARIZONA CARDINALS

Sonoran Hot Dogs

PREP TIME: 20 minutes

COOK TIME: 20 minutes

YIELD: 15 servings

15 beef hot dogs

15 slices bacon

Salt and black pepper

15 bolillo rolls (or hot dog buns)

1 cup (240 ml) mayonnaise

1 cup (195 g) canned seasoned pinto beans, drained

1 cup (180 g) diced tomatoes

1 cup (110 g) diced onions

1 cup (150 g) diced fresh or pickled jalapeños

¼ cup (60 ml) yellow mustard

¼ cup (60 ml) ketchup

¼ cup (10 g) chopped fresh cilantro

Lime wedges, for serving

The Sonoran hot dog, a regional favorite in Glendale, Arizona, has its roots in the culinary traditions of Sonora, Mexico. This indulgent creation features a hot dog wrapped in bacon, grilled to perfection, and served in a soft bolillo roll, topped with a medley of flavorful ingredients, such as pinto beans, diced tomatoes, onions, jalapeños, and an array of condiments like mustard and mayonnaise. The combination of flavors and textures reflects the fusion of Mexican and American culinary influences that characterize Arizona's regional food culture. The Sonoran hot dog can be enjoyed at various popular spots, including Tucson's renowned El Güero Canelo, famous for its authentic and delicious take on this dish.

1 Preheat a grill or skillet over medium heat. Wrap each hot dog with a slice of bacon, securing the ends with toothpicks if needed. Season the bacon-wrapped hot dogs with salt and pepper.

2 Place the hot dogs on the grill or in the skillet. Cook for 10 to 15 minutes, turning occasionally, until the bacon is crispy and the hot dogs are heated through.

3 While the hot dogs are cooking, slice the bolillo rolls in half horizontally, without cutting all the way through. If desired, toast the rolls on the grill or in a skillet over medium-high heat for a few minutes until they are lightly golden.

4 Remove the cooked hot dogs from the grill and let them rest for 1 minute, then place each one inside a roll.

5 Spread 1 tablespoon of the mayonnaise on each hot dog, then top with a spoonful of pinto beans, followed by diced tomatoes, onions, and jalapeños. Drizzle with mustard and ketchup and sprinkle with chopped cilantro.

6 Serve immediately with lime wedges for squeezing over the top.

LOS ANGELES RAMS

Sofrito Chicken Flautas

PREP TIME: 30 minutes

COOK TIME: 20 minutes

YIELD: 20 flautas

2 cups (390 g) cooked, shredded chicken

1 cup (315 g) red sofrito (I like Goya)

1 teaspoon ground cumin

1 teaspoon chili powder

1 teaspoon garlic powder

1 teaspoon onion powder

1 teaspoon salt

20 (6-inch, or 15-cm) flour tortillas

Vegetable oil, for frying

Fresh chopped cilantro, for garnishing

Sour cream, for serving

Favorite salsa, for serving

Sofrito chicken flautas are a delicious representation of the vibrant Mexican cuisine found in Los Angeles. Flautas (the word translates to "flutes" in English) are rolled tortillas typically filled with meat and then fried to crispy perfection. The use of sofrito—a flavorful blend of ingredients like onions, garlic, tomatoes, and peppers, depending on the region—enhances the chicken filling, adding depth and richness. In Los Angeles, sofrito chicken flautas can be found in various taquerias and Mexican eateries. These establishments highlight the cultural fusion of Los Angeles, where traditional dishes are celebrated and adapted to reflect the diverse culinary landscape of the city.

1 In a large bowl, combine the shredded chicken, sofrito, cumin, chili powder, garlic powder, onion powder, and salt. Mix until well combined. Taste and adjust seasoning if needed.

2 Heat a flour tortilla in a dry skillet over medium heat for 10 to 15 seconds on each side, until it is warm and pliable; this step helps prevent the tortillas from cracking when rolling.

3 Lay the warm tortilla on a flat surface. Spoon about 2 tablespoons of the chicken mixture onto the lower third of the tortilla. Roll it tightly, starting from the bottom, and tuck in the sides as you go to create a sealed cylinder. Secure the flauta with a toothpick if necessary. Repeat with the remaining tortillas and filling.

4 In a large skillet, heat about 1 inch (2.5 cm) of vegetable oil over medium-high heat until it reaches 350°F (175°C). Carefully place the flautas, in batches, in the hot oil, seam sides down, until golden brown and crispy, 3 to 4 minutes, turning occasionally to ensure even browning. Transfer to a paper towel–lined plate.

5 Arrange the flautas on a large platter. Garnish with chopped cilantro and serve with sour cream and salsa.

LOS ANGELES RAMS

French Dip Sandwiches

PREP TIME: 20 minutes

COOK TIME: 2 hours
(plus resting time)

YIELD: 12 servings

BEEF

3 pounds (1.4 kg) top round roast

Salt and black pepper

2 tablespoons olive oil

1 medium onion, thinly sliced

4 cloves garlic, minced

2 cups (480 ml) beef broth

1 cup (240 ml) water

1 tablespoon Worcestershire sauce

2 teaspoons dried thyme

2 teaspoons dried rosemary

SANDWICHES

12 French or hoagie rolls

Thinly sliced provolone or Swiss
cheese, for topping (optional)

The French dip is a beloved culinary icon in Los Angeles, known for its tender, flavorful beef and the rich, savory broth served alongside it. This sandwich traces its origins to the early twentieth century with its invention attributed to either Philippe's or Cole's, both legendary eateries in the city. Philippe's, established in 1908, asserts that the sandwich was created when a French butcher accidentally dipped a sandwich in meat juices for a customer. Cole's, a historic restaurant also founded in 1908, boasts a similar tale of origin, and the rivalry between the two establishments has become part of the sandwich's lore. At Philippe's, customers can experience the original version with its top round roast and signature French rolls, while Cole's offers a slightly different take, with its choice of slow-cooked prime rib or other meats plus options for toppings.

1 To make the beef: Preheat the oven to 325°F (165°C). Season the roast generously with salt and pepper.

2 In a large skillet, heat the olive oil over medium-high heat. Sear the roast on all sides until browned, 4 to 5 minutes per side.

3 Place the onion and garlic in a roasting pan. Pour in the beef broth and water and add the Worcestershire sauce, thyme, and rosemary. Stir to combine, then place the seared roast on top.

4 Cover the roasting pan tightly with aluminum foil and roast for 1 hour and 30 minutes to 2 hours, until the internal temperature reaches 130°F (54°C) for medium-rare, or to desired doneness. Remove the roast from the oven and let rest for 15 to 20 minutes before slicing. Increase the oven temperature to 350°F (175°C). Reserve the au jus in the pan.

5 Slice the beef thinly against the grain.

6 To make the sandwiches: Slice the rolls horizontally and place on a baking sheet. If using cheese, place a slice on each roll bottom. Toast the rolls in the oven for about 5 minutes, or until the cheese is melted and the rolls are lightly browned.

7 Place a generous portion of the beef on the bottom of each roll, then place the top of the roll. Serve with the reserved au jus from the pan for dipping.

Avocado Sourdough Toasts

PREP TIME: 15 minutes

COOK TIME: 10 minutes

YIELD: 18 toasts

AVOCADO TOAST

9 slices sourdough bread, each cut in half

3 tablespoons olive oil

6 ripe avocados

Juice of 1 lemon

Salt and black pepper

1 teaspoon red pepper flakes and/or everything bagel easoning (optional)

SUGGESTED TOPPINGS

Halved cherry tomatoes and fresh basil leaves

Slices of smoked salmon with red onions

Poached egg and hot sauce

Roasted red peppers and goat cheese

While its exact origins are debated, avocado toast has become a quintessential food trend in San Francisco (and elsewhere), where the dish reflects the city's love for fresh, locally sourced ingredients. Sourdough has a rich history that dates back to the California Gold Rush era, when the tangy bread became a staple for miners and an important part of San Francisco food culture. As evidence, the Boudin bakery still uses a starter from the region's gold mining days and the 49ers mascot is called Sourdough Sam. Sourdough also provides the perfect canvas for these toasts, enhancing their texture and flavor.

1 Preheat the oven to 400°F (205°C). Arrange the sourdough slices on two baking sheets. Brush the top of each slice with olive oil. Bake for 3 to 4 minutes, flip once, and then bake the other side until golden and crispy.

2 While the bread is toasting, cut the avocados in half, remove the pits, and scoop the flesh into a bowl. Add the lemon juice and salt and black pepper to taste and mash until smooth and creamy.

3 Spread a generous amount of mashed avocado on each slice of toast.

4 Arrange the avocado toasts on a large platter and serve immediately, garnished with red pepper flakes and/or everything bagel seasoning (if using). Serve with the suggested toppings in small bowls or on a platter for choosing.

SAN
FRANCISCO
49ERS

Mission Burritos

PREP TIME: 30 minutes

COOK TIME: 30 minutes

YIELD: 12 burritos

1 teaspoon vegetable oil

2 pounds (907 g) carne asada or chicken breast, diced medium

2 teaspoons ground cumin

2 teaspoons chili powder

Salt and black pepper

12 large (10- to 12-inch, or 25- to 30-cm) flour tortillas

2 cups (240g) shredded cheddar or Monterey Jack cheese, plus more for topping (optional)

3 cups (525 g) cooked yellow rice

1 (15-ounce, or 425-g) can black beans, rinsed and drained

1 cup (230 g) guacamole, plus more for serving (optional)

2 cups (360 g) pico de gallo (or diced tomatoes, onion, and cilantro), plus more for serving (optional)

1 cup (240 ml) sour cream

¼ cup (10 g) chopped fresh cilantro

Favorite salsa, for serving (optional)

Tortilla chips, for serving (optional)

The Mission burrito, a culinary staple of San Francisco, originated in the Mission District during the 1960s and '70s, a time when the neighborhood was a vibrant hub of Mexican culture and immigration. This substantial burrito was designed to be a portable meal for workers and has since become synonymous with California-style Mexican cuisine. The burrito typically features a flour tortilla filled with ingredients such as rice, beans, meat, cheese, and salsa, allowing for a customizable dining experience that caters to diverse tastes. Two iconic places known for serving delicious Mission burritos are La Taqueria and Taqueria El Farolito.

1 In a large skillet, heat the vegetable oil over medium-high heat. Add the diced meat and cook until fully cooked and browned, 10 to 12 minutes for carne asada and 8 to 10 minutes for chicken. Season with the cumin, chili powder, and salt and pepper to taste.

2 Heat a flour tortilla in a dry skillet over medium heat for 10 to 15 seconds on each side, until it is warm and pliable. Spread an even layer of cheese along the center of the tortilla, then spread some rice over the cheese. Spoon some beans on top of the rice, followed by additional cheese, then the meat, guacamole, pico de gallo, sour cream, and cilantro.

3 Fold in the sides of the tortilla, then roll it from the bottom up to form a burrito. Ensure the filling is fully enclosed. Repeat for the remaining tortillas and fillings.

4 Heat a large skillet over medium-high heat. Place the assembled burritos, seam sides down, in batches, to crisp the outsides for 2 to 3 minutes per side. If desired, sprinkle extra cheese on top and cover the pan to melt.

5 Cut the burritos in half, if desired, and serve with additional pico de gallo, guacamole, and/or salsa. You can also serve with tortilla chips.

SEATTLE SEAHAWKS

Smoked Salmon Chowder

PREP TIME: 20 minutes

COOK TIME: 40 minutes

YIELD: 20 servings

¼ cup (55 g, or ½ stick) unsalted butter

1 large onion, small diced

4 ribs celery, small diced

4 carrots, small diced

4 cloves garlic, minced

8 cups (1.9 kg) chicken or vegetable broth

4 medium red potatoes, peeled and medium diced

2 cups (480 ml) heavy cream

1 cup (135 g) frozen corn kernels

2 cups (270 g) chopped hot-smoked salmon (cut into ¼-inch, or 6 mm, pieces)

1 teaspoon dried thyme

1 teaspoon dried dill

1 teaspoon black pepper

2 teaspoons kosher salt, or to taste

1 tablespoon fresh lemon juice

Chopped fresh dill or flat-leaf parsley, for garnishing (optional)

Smoked salmon chowder highlights the fresh, rich flavors of the Pacific Northwest. Its origins can be traced back to the region's fishing culture in which salmon was a staple ingredient. The chowder combines a creamy broth with chunks of hot-smoked salmon, potatoes, and vegetables, and its appeal lies in its comforting texture and smoky flavor. Pike Place Chowder, located in the iconic Pike Place Market, is renowned for its chowder varieties, including their acclaimed smoked salmon chowder, which showcases locally sourced ingredients and has won numerous awards.

1 In a large stockpot, melt the butter over medium heat. Add the onion, celery, and carrots and cook, stirring often, for 5 to 7 minutes, until the vegetables are softened.

2 Stir in the garlic and cook for an additional minute, or until fragrant. Add the broth and potatoes to the pot. Bring to a boil, then reduce the heat and let simmer over medium-high heat for 15 minutes, or until the potatoes are tender.

3 Stir in the cream, corn, salmon, thyme, dill, pepper, and salt. Let simmer for an additional 5 to 10 minutes, until heated through.

4 Remove the chowder from heat and stir in the lemon juice. Adjust the seasoning with more salt and/or pepper if needed. Serve hot, garnished with chopped dill or parsley (if using).

SEATTLE
SEAHAWKS

Teriyaki Chicken

PREP TIME: 15 minutes, plus 1 hour marinating

COOK TIME: 15 to 25 minutes

YIELD: 15 servings

2 cups (480 ml) soy sauce

1½ cups (360 ml) mirin (sweet rice wine)

1½ cups (330 g) brown sugar

1 tablespoon grated fresh ginger

2 tablespoons minced garlic

1 teaspoon sesame oil

1 teaspoon black pepper

7½ pounds (3.4 kg) boneless, skinless chicken thighs

1½ tablespoons cornstarch

3 tablespoons water

Cooked white rice, for serving

Sesame seeds, for garnishing

Chopped scallions, for garnishing

Teriyaki chicken has become an iconic dish in Seattle, reflecting the city's diverse culinary influences, particularly from its Japanese American community. "Teriyaki" refers to a traditional Japanese cooking method that involves grilling or broiling meat with a glaze made from soy sauce, sake, and sugar. In 1976, Toshi Kasahara, a Japanese American chef and longtime Seattle resident, opened Seattle's first teriyaki joint near the Space Needle, introducing locals to his chargrilled, smoky-sweet chicken. One of the best long-standing places for the dish in the Seattle area is Toshio's Teriyaki, which has been serving up delicious teriyaki dishes since the early 1980s.

1 In a large bowl, whisk together the soy sauce, mirin, brown sugar, ginger, garlic, sesame oil, and pepper until well combined.

2 Place the chicken thighs in a large resealable plastic bag or shallow dish. Reserve 1 cup (240 ml) of the marinade for later use, then pour the remaining marinade over the chicken, making sure it is well coated. Seal the bag or cover the dish and refrigerate for at least 1 hour, or overnight for better flavor.

3 If grilling, preheat the grill to medium-high heat. If using an oven, preheat it to 400°F (205°C). Remove the chicken from the marinade and discard the used marinade. If grilling, cook the chicken thighs for 6 to 7 minutes on each side, until fully cooked (internal temperature should reach 165°F, or 75°C). If using the oven, place the marinated chicken on a baking sheet lined with parchment paper. Bake for 25 to 30 minutes, until fully cooked (internal temperature should reach 165°F, or 75°C).

4 Combine the reserved marinade with the cornstarch and water in a small saucepan. Cook over medium heat, stirring until the sauce thickens.

5 Once the chicken is cooked, remove it from the heat and let rest for a few minutes before slicing. Serve the sliced teriyaki chicken over cooked white rice, drizzled with the sauce. Garnish with sesame seeds and chopped scallions.

Team Tidbits

Brush up on the facts of your favorite team, discover the roots of another team's fandom, or prove to your rival-loving friends that you know more about their team than they do with these quick-study overviews of all 32 pro teams.

AFC NORTH

BALTIMORE RAVENS

Year Established: 1996

Mascot(s): Poe (costumed), Rise (live), and Conquer (live), ravens

Colors: Black, purple, white, and gold

Fight Song: "The Baltimore Fight Song"

Traditions: Fans and players rub the toes of the statues of Ray Lewis and Johnny Unitas located at the entrance of the Ravens' stadium for good luck.

Hometown Fun Fact: "The Star-Spangled Banner" was written in Baltimore by Francis Scott Key, who was a prisoner in Fort McHenry.

CINCINNATI BENGALS

Year Established: 1967

Mascot(s): Who Dey, a Bengal tiger

Colors: Orange, black, and white

Fight Song: "The Bengal Growl"

Traditions: The Bengals fans' chant "Who Dey" has become synonymous with the team.

Hometown Fun Fact: Cincinnati is home to the second oldest zoo in America, the Cincinnati Zoo & Botanical Gardens.

CLEVELAND BROWNS

Year Established: 1946

Mascot(s): Chomps and Brownie (costumed), a labrador and an elf; Muni and Stripes (live), bullmastiffs

Colors: Dark brown, orange, and white.

Traditions: The Browns' home stadium has a dedicated fan section called the Dawg Pound. Fans are famous for their Dawg Pound Bark (barking after big plays).

Hometown Fun Fact: Cleveland is home to many important cultural institutions such as the Rock and Roll Hall of Fame, the Cleveland Museum of Natural History, and the Cleveland Museum of Art, which earned it the designation of a global city by the Globalization and World Cities Research Network.

Fan Nickname(s): Dawg Pound, Browns Backers Worldwide

PITTSBURGH STEELERS

Year Established: 1933

Mascot(s): Steely McBeam, a steelworker

Colors: Black and Steeler's Gold

Fight Song: "Renegade" by Styx (played during the fourth quarter), "Black and Yellow" by Wiz Khalifa

Traditions: Steelers fans spin yellow towels, referred to as the Terrible Towel, at home games. The Terrible Towel has become so synonymous with Pittsburgh Pride that Steelers fans have brought their Towels to the peak of Mount Everest and onto the International Space Station.

Hometown Fun Fact: The Steelers' name is a reference to Pittsburgh's historically significant role in the US steel industry.

Fan Nickname(s): Steeler Nation

 In 1943 due to player shortages caused by World War II the two Pennsylvania football teams joined forces to form the Phil-Pitt Combine, also known as the Steagles.

AFC SOUTH

HOUSTON TEXANS

Year Established: 2002

Mascot(s): Toro, a bull

Colors: Deep steel blue, battle red, liberty white, and H-Town blue

Fight Songs: "Football Time in Houston" and Chevelle's "Hats off to the Bulls"

Traditions: The Texans' fan section, known as the Bull Pen, has quickly become one of the rowdiest in the NFL.

Hometown Fun Fact: Houston is home to NASA's Johnson Space Center and the Mission Control Center.

 DID YOU KNOW? The Texans were established after the Houston Oilers moved to Nashville to become the Tennessee Titans.

INDIANAPOLIS COLTS

Year Established: 1953

Mascot(s): Blue, a horse

Colors: Speed Blue, grey, white, and black

Traditions: Introduced in 2017, the Colts strike an anvil before the start of home games, symbolizing the strength of their fans and relating to their horseshoe logo.

Hometown Fun Fact: Indianapolis's official motto is "Crossroad of America" due to its historical role as a major hub of transportation.

 DID YOU KNOW? The Colts were originally Baltimore's team but relocated to Indy in 1984.

JACKSONVILLE JAGUARS

Year Established: 1995

Mascot(s): Jaxson de Ville, a jaguar

Colors: Teal, black, gold, and white

Traditions: Fans chant "Duval" to express both pride for their team and Jacksonville itself, which is located in Duval County.

Hometown Fun Fact: Jacksonville, Florida is named after Andrew Jackson, the seventh president of the United States.

Fan Nickname(s): Duval

TENNESSEE TITANS

Year Established: 1960

Mascot(s): T-Rac, a racoon.

Colors: Titans navy, Titans blue, red, silver, and white

Fight Song: "Get Loud (Titan Up)" by OUTSKRTS

Traditions: Lucky fans get to plunge the Sword of Honor into the field to mark the Titans' territory. In 2023, the Titans switched to a turf field, so an elaborate prop was introduced to carry on this tradition.

Hometown Fun Fact: Nashville, Tennessee, is nicknamed "Music City" as it is a hub for the music industry with a thriving country music scene.

 DID YOU KNOW? After moving to Tennessee in 1997, the team remained the Oilers until 1999 when they officially became the Titans.

AFC EAST

BUFFALO BILLS

Year Established: 1959

Mascot(s): Billy Buffalo, a blue bison

Colors: Royal blue, red, white, and grey

Fight Songs: "Shout" by the Isley Brothers and "Mr. Brightside" by the Killers

Traditions: Bills fans are well known for the pre-game tradition of table jumping, where they will jump on top of folding tables, often from high places like the tops of cars, RVs, and port-a-potties, the goal being to break through the plastic furniture.

Hometown Fun Fact: Buffalo was the first US city to have electrically lit streets in 1886. More recently the city is widely known for its chicken wings, which were invented in 1964 at the Anchor Bar.

Fan Nickname(s): Bills Mafia, Bills Backers

 DID YOU KNOW? While the Bills don't get their name from their city (they are named after frontiersman Buffalo Bill), they are the only NFL team to play their home games in the state of New York; the other New York teams, the Jets and the Giants, play in New Jersey.

MIAMI DOLPHINS

Year Established: 1966

Mascot(s): T. D., a dolphin

Colors: Aqua, orange, marine blue, and white

Fight Song: The Miami Dolphins have an official, classic fight song written by Lee Offman in 1972, though Jimmy Buffet's "Fins" is also used.

Traditions: Dolphins fans still honor their undefeated 1972 season by singing the 1972 fight song by Lee Offman.

Hometown Fun Fact: Miami has sometimes been referred to as the "Gateway to Latin America" due to the strong presence of Latin American culture in and around the city.

Fan nicknames: DolFans, The Pod

NEW ENGLAND PATRIOTS

Year Established: 1959

Mascot(s): Pat Patriot, a revolutionary war soldier

Colors: Nautical blue, red, New Century silver, and white

Fight Song: "I'm Shipping Up to Boston" by the Dropkick Murphys

Traditions: After Patriot touchdowns during home games, the end zone militia in their 1800s garb fires muskets in celebration. Patriots fans are also famous for their "Do Your Job" chant.

Hometown Fun Fact: Boston is home to many historical events, perhaps the most notorious being the Boston Tea Party.

 DID YOU KNOW? The Patriots were originally founded as the Boston Patriots but became the more inclusive New England Patriots when they moved to Foxborough.

NEW YORK JETS

Year Established: 1959

Mascot(s): While not an official mascot, Fireman Ed (superfan Edwin Anzalone) leads the fans in the famous Jets chant.

Colors: Gotham Green, Stealth Black, and Legacy White

Fight Song: "J-E-T-S, Jets! Jets! Jets!" chant

Traditions: Jets fans are famous for their simple and recognizable chant, where they enthusiastically spell out the team's name.

Hometown Fun Fact: New York has around 800 different languages being spoken within its borders, the most of any city in the world.

 DID YOU KNOW? The Jets were originally named the Titans of New York. They got their current team name when they were sold in 1963.

AFC WEST

DENVER BRONCOS

Year Established: 1959

Mascot(s): Miles (costumed), Thunder (live), horses

Colors: Midnight Navy, Sunset Orange, and Summit White

Traditions: Broncos fans and players perform the "Mile High Salute" to celebrate touchdowns. The celebration was popularized by player Terrell Davis to honor the military in the 1990s.

Hometown Fun Fact: Denver is commonly referred to has the "Mile High City" as its elevation above sea level is exactly one mile. Three of the five longest field goals in NFL history have happened in Denver, thanks to the thin air of the high-elevation city.

KANSAS CITY CHIEFS

Year Established: 1960

Mascot(s): K. C. Wolf, a gray wolf

Colors: Red, gold, white, and black.

Traditions: Historically Chiefs fans have performed the "Arrowhead Chop," but the club is currently looking for more respectful and inclusive ways to celebrate their team's victories.

Hometown Fun Fact: Kansas City is nicknamed the "City of Fountains" due to its many fountains, which are a significant part of the city's culture. The first fountains were installed in the late 1800s to provide drinking water for people, horses, and birds.

Fan Nickname(s): Chiefs Kingdom

DID YOU KNOW? Originally Texas-based and known as the Dallas Texans, when the team moved to Missouri in 1963, they rebranded as the Kansas City Chiefs.

LAS VEGAS RAIDERS

Year Established: 1960

Mascot(s): The Raider Rusher, an animated character from the cartoon series *NFL Rush Zone*

Colors: Black and silver

Fight Song: "The Autumn Wind"

Traditions: Raiders fans are famous for "The Black Hole" section, where fans dress in elaborate costumes, often including skull face paint.

Hometown Fun Fact: Las Vegas is the largest city in Nevada and is renowned for its booming entertainment industry including resorts, casinos, restaurants, and shopping centers.

Fan Nickname(s): Raider Nation

DID YOU KNOW? The Raiders called both Oakland and Los Angeles home before their 2020 move to Las Vegas.

LOS ANGELES CHARGERS

Year Established: 1959

Mascot(s): The Chargers do not have an official mascot, but they did have Boltman, brought to life by Dan Jauregui for twenty-two years before retiring in 2018.

Colors: Powder Blue, Sunshine Gold, and white

Fight Song: "Bolt Up!" chant

Traditions: Chargers fans chant while mimicking lightning bolts with their arms to energize the stadium and the players.

Hometown Fun Fact: Los Angeles is often referred to as the "City of Angels" in homage to the city's original Spanish name, El Pueblo de Nuestra Señora la Reina de los Ángeles (The Town of Our Lady the Queen of the Angels).

DID YOU KNOW? The Chargers left LA due to competition with the Rams. They relocated to San Diego in 1961 before heading back up the I-5 in 2017.

NFC

NFC NORTH

CHICAGO BEARS

Year Established: 1920

Mascot(s): Staley Da Bear, a brown bear

Colors: Dark navy, orange, and white

Fight Song: "Bear Down, Chicago Bears"

Traditions: Fans call the team "Da Bears." 1985's "The Super Bowl Shuffle" was recorded by the players (credited as the Chicago Bears Shufflin' Crew) who would go on to win Super Bowl XX after a dream one-loss regular season. The song, which peaked at number 41 on the US Billboard Hot 100 and earned a Grammy nomination, is still beloved by fans today.

Hometown Fun Fact: Chicago, also known as "The Windy City," is known for its icons—deep-dish pizza, The Bean, Wrigley Field, and Willis Tower

DID YOU KNOW? The Bears' longest standing rivalry is with the Arizona Cardinals, who they played for the first time in 1920.

DETROIT LIONS

Year Established: 1930

Mascot(s): Roary, a lion

Colors: Honolulu Blue, silver, white, and black.

Fight Song: "Gridiron Heroes"

Traditions: The tradition of the Lions playing on Thanksgiving Day started in 1934 and they have played almost every holiday since.

Hometown Fun Fact: Detroit is famous for its ties to the automotive industry and its distinctive Motown music style and sound from the 1960s.

DID YOU KNOW? The team was originally located in Ohio, playing as the Portsmouth Spartans, until they were bought and moved to Detroit in 1934 where they became the Lions.

GREEN BAY PACKERS

Year Established: 1919

Mascot(s): The Packers don't have an official mascot, but the cheese wedge-shaped hats that fans wear to games are good stand ins.

Colors: Dark green, gold, and white

Fight Song: "Go! You Packers Go!"

Traditions: The Super Bowl trophy is named after Vince Lombardi, who acted as head coach of the Packers from 1959 to 1967. The Packers started the tradition of the Lambeau Leap—celebrating a touchdown by jumping into the stands behind the end zone. The Leap has been adopted by players across the league and performed for years.

Hometown Fun Fact: Green Bay is home to the National Railroad Museum and Lambeau field, which still acts as home to the Packers.

Fan Nickname(s): Cheeseheads

 DID YOU KNOW? The Green Bay Packers are a community-owned, non-profit team, and the only professional sports team in the United States with that status.

MINNESOTA VIKINGS

Year Established: 1961

Mascot(s): Victor, a Viking

Colors: Purple, gold, and white

Fight Song: "Skol, Vikings"

Traditions: Before each home game, a mythical Norse horn called a Gjallarhorn is blown. Fans also chant skol (cheers or good health) to a drum beat during games.

Hometown Fun Fact: Minneapolis and neighboring St. Paul are known as the "Twin Cities" and Minneapolis is nicknamed the "City of Lakes" as it is home to thirteen lakes, the Mississippi River, wetlands, waterfalls, and creeks.

NFC SOUTH

ATLANTA FALCONS

Year Established: 1965

Mascot(s): Freddie, a falcon

Colors: Red, black, white, and silver.

Fight Song: The Falcons don't have an official fight song, but "Welcome to Atlanta" has been adopted by the fans, who also chant "Rise Up!" and the "In Brotherhood" team rallying cry.

Traditions: The general admission section of State Farm Stadium is named the Dirty Birds Nest. The nickname originates with Jamal Anderson's famous Dirty Bird Dance, which fans happily recreate as well.

Hometown Fun Fact: Atlanta owes much of its early history to the railways that were built through the city in 1830s. The city was originally named Terminus in reference to the southern end of a Western and Atlantic Railroad railway, and it was dubbed Atlanta as a feminine version of Atlantic by the chief engineer of the Georgia Railroad.

Fan Nickname(s): Dirty Birds

 DID YOU KNOW? The Falcons' red, black, and white colors were chosen to unite with and represent the two most well-known college football teams in Georgia at the time, Georgia Tech and the University of Georgia.

CAROLINA PANTHERS

Year Established: 1993

Mascot(s): Sir Purr, a black panther

Colors: Process Blue, black, and silver.

Fight Song: "Stand and Cheer"

Traditions: Inspired by the iconic 2003 speech by former Panther linebacker and assistant coach Sam Mills who passed away from cancer in 2005, the team started the tradition of the "Keep Pounding" drum and chant before home games.

Hometown Fun Fact: Charlotte, North Carolina is known for being a cultural hub and the most populous city in North Carolina.

Fan Nickname(s): Panthers fans don't have an official nickname, though they do have a thriving fan club named the Roaring Riot.

NEW ORLEANS SAINTS

Year Established: 1966

Mascot(s): Sir Saint, a player in uniform, and Gumbo, a St. Bernard

Colors: Black, Old Gold, and white

Fight Song: "When the Saints Go Marching In"

Traditions: "Who Dat?" chant

Hometown Fun Fact: New Orleans is known for its Creole cuisine, unique dialects, above-ground cemeteries, and annual celebrations and festivals. It is also the birthplace of jazz music and jazz funerals, the latter being closely connected to the city's celebratory embrace of death.

Fan Nickname(s): Who Dat Nation

 The Saints became New Orlean's football team on November 1, All Saints Day.

TAMPA BAY BUCCANEERS

Year Established: 1976

Mascot(s): Captain Fear, a Caribbean pirate captain

Colors: Red, black, orange, white, and pewter

Fight Song: "Hey! Hey! Tampa Bay!"

Traditions: A pirate ship within the Buccaneers' home stadium fires a canon for each point the team scores.

Hometown Fun Fact: The first recordings of the name "Tampa Bay" ("Bahía Tampa") occurred hundreds of years ago, with one of the firsts being in 1576.

NFC EAST

DALLAS COWBOYS

Year Established: 1960

Mascot(s): Rowdy, a cowboy

Colors: Blue, silver, and white

Fight Song: "How 'Bout Them Boys" chant

Traditions: The Dallas Cowboys Cheerleaders are an international phenomenon known for their impact on pop culture, iconic uniforms, and choreography. The Cowboys are the only NFL team to wear white during home games due to the heat of Texas.

Hometown Fun Fact: Dallas has one of the busiest and most-visited airports in the world, Dallas Fort Worth International Airport.

 The Cowboys had 20 consecutive winning seasons from 1966 to 1985, the most of any NFL team.

NEW YORK GIANTS

Year Established: 1925

Colors: Dark blue, red, white, and grey

Traditions: The New York Giants are known as "Big Blue" to their fans. Before home games, AC/DC's "Hells Bells" is played.

Hometown Fun Fact: New York City is America's its most populated city, with nearly twice the residents of the next largest city, Los Angeles.

 The Giants are still a family-owned team, with the current owner John Mara being the grandson of the original owner.

PHILADELPHIA EAGLES

Year Established: 1933

Mascot(s): Swoop (costumed), Lincoln (live), eagles

Colors: Midnight Green, white, black, and silver

Fight Song: "Fly, Eagles, Fly," "E-A-G-L-E-S, EAGLES!" chant, and "Go Birds!" rallying cry

Traditions: The team is referred to by fans as "The Birds" or "The Iggles." And when the team wins major games, fans flock to the main artery of the city, Broad Street, and climb to the highest point, which is usually the top of streetlights.

Hometown Fun Fact: Philadelphia has a deep connection to US history and is the home of many important historical moments and icons, like the Liberty Bell and the signing of the Declaration of Independence. The city is also the location of the iconic Rocky movie franchise; a statue of Sylvester Stallone's character stands at the bottom of the famous steps of the Philadelphia Museum of Art.

Fan Nickname(s): Bird Call, Bird Gang, Boo Birds

 Between 1997 and 2003 the Eagles appointed a judge to preside over "Eagles Court," a temporary courtroom (complete with jail cell!) within their stadium to deal with overly zealous fans.

WASHINGTON COMMANDERS

Year Established: 1932

Mascot(s): Major Tuddy, a hog/pig

Colors: Burgandy, gold, white, and black

Fight Song: "Hail to the Commanders"

Traditions: The Commanders were the first NFL team to have a marching band, radio network, and fully televised season. The band plays the fight song after every touchdown.

Hometown Fun Fact: Washington, DC's National Cathedral building has many gargoyles and one of them is the sculpted head of Darth Vader on the northwest tower. Also the city's metro is the second busiest in the country, after New York City.

 DID YOU KNOW? The team was originally founded in Boston and played as the Boston Braves until 1937 when they relocated to Washington, DC and were renamed.

NFC WEST

ARIZONA CARDINALS

Year Established: 1898

Mascot(s): Big Red, a cardinal

Colors: Cardinal Red, black, white, and silver

Fight Song: "Cardinals are Charging"

Hometown Fun Fact: Phoenix is perhaps best known for its year-round sunshine, but it's also home to one of the largest municipal parks in North America as well as the college football Fiesta and Rate Bowls.

Fan Nickname(s): The Red Sea

 DID YOU KNOW? The Cardinals are the oldest professional football club in the NFL.

LOS ANGELES RAMS

Year Established: 1936

Mascot(s): Rampage, a ram

Colors: Ram's Royal Blue, Sol Yellow, gold, and white

Traditions: Rams fans often attend games wearing hollowed out watermelons on their heads.

Hometown Fun Fact: Los Angeles has the shortest street in the world (Powers Place, 13 feet, 3.9 m) and one of the longest (Sepulveda Boulevard, 42.8 miles, 68,879 m).

Fan nicknames: Mob Squad, The Herd, Ramily, Ramilia, and Ram's Nation

 DID YOU KNOW? The Rams were the first NFL team to have a logo when player Fred Gehrke painted horns on his helmet in the 1940s, which the Rams quickly officially adopted.

SAN FRANCISCO 49ERS

Year Established: 1949

Mascot(s): Sourdough Sam, a gold miner

Colors: 49ers Red, gold, white, and black

Fight Song: "Bang! Bang! Niner Gang!" chant

Traditions: A foghorn sounds before the start of games, at halftime, and after touchdowns.

Hometown Fun Fact: The fortune cookie and the Mission Style burrito were both created in San Francisco. And the city's famous fog has a name—Karl!

Fan nicknames: 49er Faithful, the Niner Gang, the Niner Empire

 DID YOU KNOW? The 49ers are the first major league sports team to be located in San Francisco.

SEATTLE SEAHAWKS

Year Established: 1976

Mascot(s): Blitz and Boom (costumed), blue birds, and Taima (live), an augur buzzard

Colors: College Navy, Action Green, and Wolf Gray

Traditions: Seahawks fans are considered to be one of the loudest groups of fans in the NFL, setting the record for the loudest crowd noise at a sporting event twice and causing well over a hundred false start penalties for opposing teams between 2002 and 2012.

Hometown Fun Fact: Many prominent technology companies have called Seattle home over the years, including Boeing, which was founded in Seattle, and Microsoft.

Fan Nickname(s): The 12th Man or the 12s

Index

ACKNOWLEDGMENTS

The idea of exploring food culture has been something I've been passionate about throughout my entire career as a chef. But I learned the most about it during my fourteen years working for one of the greatest football organizations in the NFL—the Philadelphia Eagles. Every day in that kitchen, working alongside the best kitchen crew, I had the privilege of cooking for players, coaches, and staff who fueled my passion for food and deepened my appreciation for how it brings people together. Thank you to my former coworkers for your dedication, your talent, and the countless good times shared behind the line.

I also want to thank the many players, coaches, and staff members who gave me insight into their food traditions, preferences, and cultures. Learning about what comforted, energized, and inspired them on and off the field helped shape the way I think about game-day food. This book wouldn't exist without that experience.

To my culinary students at Jules E. Mastbaum High School in Philadelphia—you remind me every day why I love cooking, teaching, and learning in the kitchen. Your enthusiasm, curiosity, and creativity push me to be better, and I hope this book serves as a reminder that great food is for everyone, no matter where you come from.

And finally, to my family—my wife, Melissa, and my son, Parker. Melissa, your unwavering support, patience, and belief in me make everything I do possible. You are my best critic and my biggest cheerleader. Parker, you remind me every day of why cooking for my family is so important. Watching you grow and teaching you to value the simple things like sharing a meal together—it fuels me in ways I can't describe. This book, this journey, all of it, is for you both.

ABOUT THE AUTHOR

Tim Lopez has been a chef for over twenty-five years. He has worked at various restaurants and country clubs and in corporate dining for an NFL football team. While working at this job, he became invested in the food culture of players, coaches, and fans throughout the league.

Tim has a passion for regional cuisine and enjoys exploring all the foods the United States has to offer. He is currently a culinary arts teacher in Philadelphia, Pennsylvania. He lives in southern New Jersey with his wife, Melissa, a literacy teacher, his son, Parker, and their two dogs.